COLDWATER & TEMPERATE

FISH KEEPING FOR BEGINNERS

JUNIOR EDITION

FLO AQUARIA

FLO AQUARIA

COLDWATER
& TEMPERATE
FISH KEEPING
FOR BEGINNERS

EASY WEEK BY WEEK GUIDE

JUNIOR EDITION
COMPLETE SET-UP, MAINTENANCE, MONITORING & CARE GUIDE INCLUDING LOG BOOK

FLO
Aquaria

FISH CARE MADE EASY

LITTLE NEMO

YOU MAY HAVE ONLY ONE PECTORAL FIN

BUT YOU NEVER SWIM IN CIRCLES

KEEP GOING

AND

KEEP GROWING

FLO AQUARIA

CONTENTS

INTRODUCTION

Keeping any pet is a great responsibility as you may already know.

In time you will want to be able to look after your fish and aquarium yourself.

If, or when, you are ready, your responsible adult will let you know what they are happy for you to do on your own.

Some parts of this book will be just for you to read and complete on your own, and others will be for you and your responsible adult to read and understand together.

Take care, have fun and most importantly of all BE SAFE.

We recommend you and your responsible adult, read the whole of this guide before you begin setting up your aquarium.

FLO AQUARIA

CHAPTER 1

WHAT ARE COLDWATER AND

TEMPERATE FISH?

This guide is specific to Coldwater & Temperate fish keeping (fish keeping without aquarium heaters).

Fish, such as Goldfish (excluding most fancy varieties), can live and thrive indoors in aquariums or outdoors in ponds.

Their range of tolerable water temperatures (temperatures they can survive within) is quite broad; for example, in a pond they can survive temperatures down to almost freezing, but will quite happily live in an aquarium at temperatures up to 29°C.

For this reason we consider them to be a temperate (not strictly coldwater) species.

Fancy Goldfish and some of the other varieties we discuss will be ideally suited to the higher range of these temperatures yet still below the temperatures of a fully heated "tropical aquarium".

In a home that is heated to be comfortable for its human occupants, temperate fish will live quite happily in unheated/ room temperature water, of around 20-23°C.

All fish species have slightly different desired temperature ranges; you will find that these ranges overlap around the temperature noted above for the temperate varieties.

This makes them suitable for an unheated aquarium, in a home or space that is heated properly for the seasons of the year.

CHAPTER 2

SIMPLE FISH ANATOMY

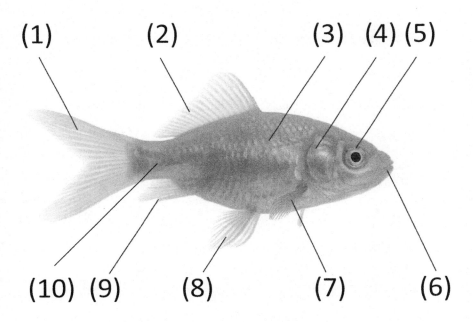

(1) (2) (3) (4) (5)

(10) (9) (8) (7) (6)

1) Caudal Fin

Often referred to as the tail fin; the caudal fin is use to propel the fish forward in the water as it swims.

2) Dorsal Fin

Keeps the fish upright and gives it stability in the water.

3) Lateral Line

A line of sensory pits that run along the side of the fish, starting from behind the gill plate and stretching horizontally towards the caudal fin.

The lateral line helps the fish to sense vibrations within the water and changes in water pressure.

4) Gill Covers

Covers and protects the Gills.

Located on each side of the Fish. The gills assist fish to filter and remove dissolved oxygen from the water and return Carbon Dioxide into the water.

5) Eyes

Used to see the underwater world.

6) Mouth

Perfect for eating food and taking water in that will be passed through the gills.

7) Pectoral Fins

Positioned on either side of the fish below and behind the gill cover.

The pectoral fins are used for small movements forward and backwards within the water.

8) Pelvic Fins

Used for stability and steering,

The pelvic fins are located on either side of the fish between the pectoral and anal fins.

9) Anal Fin

A single fin situated below the caudal fin.

10) Scales

Covering the skin on most fish species (scale-less fish do exist).

These tiny, soft, bone plates protect the fish from predators and parasites like a delicate chainmail coat of armour.

CHAPTER 3

WHAT TEMPERATE FISH CAN I

KEEP IN MY AQUARIUM?

We have broken our list of suggestions into two categories; Starter and Intermediate.

As you are just starting your aquarium we recommend you selecting from the starter fish list.

This should give you hardier fish that will help you mature your first aquarium.

Take time to research each the varieties listed and you will be amazed by the significant differences of each.

Starter Fish

- Common Goldfish

- Platys

- Pearl Danios

- White Cloud Minnows

- Guppies

- Endlers Livebearer

- Rosy Barbs (Please note Rosy Barbs can be kept at this temperature but can nip the fins of longer fin species and so may be best kept in a single species only aquarium).

Intermediate fish

- Fancy Goldfish

We consider that Fancy Goldfish should stand in a category of their own as Intermediate Fish.

Fancy Goldfish may be kept in your unheated aquarium but will be harder for you as a first-time fish keeper.

This is because they are typically more sensitive to water quality and would be less hardy to the unstable conditions of a new aquarium.

They are definitely something you will want to consider as you progress within the hobby.

Look into the following fancy varieties and you will be amazed.

Shubunkins, Comets, Fantails, Orandas, Bubble Eyes, Celestials, Lionheads, Black Moors,

We could continue and the list would be potentially endless with colour and tail variations.

A BRIEF HISTORY OF GOLDFISH

Goldfish (Carassius Auratus) were first selectively bred for colour over 1000 years ago in their native home of Imperial China.

Originally fish were kept as a food source however, through variations in breeding, fish with more coloured, shiny scales were noticed and from these fish selective breeding began.

A small closely related member of the carp family, the goldfish we love today, with its bright colours and many varieties, would have at one time been a much more modest looking fish.

Though your choice of fish is not limited to Goldfish alone, at present day they are still one of the world's most popularly kept fish.

Even with the huge range of alternatives choices the Common Goldfish is still a great favourite amongst beginners to the hobby.

Fish keeping has been popular, for different reasons, for thousands of years and you are now a small part of that history.

CHAPTER 4

THE KEY ELEMENTS OF YOUR

AQUARIUM

Your aquarium will consist of a **TANK** made from glass or acrylic that will hold the water, decorations and fish.

The fish waste will be cleaned from the water of the tank with the help of your **FILTER**.

The filter sucks water and waste in and the waste will be caught inside the filter in sponges.

This is known as Mechanical Filtration.

Bacteria that grow inside of the tank in the gravel, in the water, and on the filter sponges, acts to clean the water of harmful fish waste by a process known as the Nitrogen Cycle.

This is known as <u>Biological Filtration</u>.

Fish breathe dissolved oxygen from the water as it passes through their gills and because of this the oxygen level in the water will decrease.

You will use an **AIR PUMP** located on the outside of your tank and it will feed air down an air-hose into your tank.

On the tank end of your air-line you will attach an air-stone and when the air passes through the air-stone it will diffuse, creating bubbles in the water that will rise to the surface.

When these bubbles break the surface of the water, they will allow oxygen to be dissolved into the water of the aquarium.

This will replace the oxygen that is being used by your fish.

You should also have a **LIGHT** on your aquarium that will enable you to see your fish clearer.

By turning the light on and off at the right times you can re-create the natural day and night light cycle that fish would experience in nature.

CHAPTER 5

THE NITROGEN CYCLE

EXPLAINED

Just what is the Nitrogen Cycle?

Sometimes known as the Water Cycle, the Nitrogen Cycle is a hidden cycle of waste and naturally occurring bacteria in your aquarium.

Each part of the cycle helps and supports the next; the success of any one part of the cycle is dependent on the success of each other part, for success to be achieved as a whole.

Why does this matter to me if I can't see it?

Given the right conditions for the Nitrogen Cycle to occur, it will help keep your aquarium water healthy and suitable for your fish to live in.

Tell me more, this sounds complicated?

It is nothing to be worried about, when you follow the instructions given and give the right care nature will do the rest.

Let us explain;

The cycle begins with Ammonia.

When fish eat, quite like you and I, they produce waste.

We go to the toilet, but the waste that your fish produce is deposited into the water of your aquarium.

This fish waste, along with uneaten food, will produce Ammonia in the water which is poisonous to your fish.

The chemical symbol for Ammonia is NH_3

So you must feed your fish, but when you do you are adding to the Ammonia?

Correct, but fortunately for us as fish keepers, we also keep naturally occurring bacteria hidden in our aquarium that lives to feed on this Ammonia.

Given the right conditions, this bacteria exists within the water, particularly amongst the gravel and on your filter media and is known as Nitrosonoma.

The Nitrosonoma bacteria will grow in strength where Ammonia exists.

They consume the toxic Ammonia but the waste that they then produce goes back into the water as another chemical, Nitrite.

The chemical symbol for Nitrite is NO_2.

Nitrite is only <u>slightly</u> less toxic than Ammonia and is still harmful to fish so we have swapped one harmful chemical for another.

At this stage we need to introduce you to another helpful naturally occurring bacteria, in the form of Nitrobacter.

The Nitrobacter will feed on the Nitrite in the aquarium and the waste product of this process is another chemical, the <u>almost harmless</u> Nitrate.

The chemical symbol for Nitrate is NO_3.

Nitrate is much less harmful to your fish than both the highly toxic Ammonia and Nitrite, if kept at manageable levels.

FLO AQUARIA

THE NITROGEN CYCLE IN NATURE Vs THE NITROGEN CYCLE IN AN AQUARIUM

To make it easier for you to visualise, we have compared the Nitrogen Cycle in Nature with the Nitrogen Cycle in an Aquarium using two diagrams.

They are slightly different and we will explain why on the next pages.

The Nitrogen Cycle in Nature

In nature the Nitrate waste from the whole cycle would likely be far less concentrated and would also be used up as a source of food for plants within the water.

Fish would then eat the plants and the cycle would repeat.

See Figure 1 for a simple illustration of the Nitrogen Cycle in Nature.

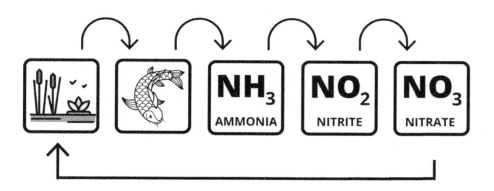

Figure 1: The Nitrogen Cycle in Nature

The Nitrogen Cycle in an Aquarium

In an aquarium we start the cycle, by feeding, and vary the cycle, by performing partial water changes, to reduce and dilute the Nitrate.

These water changes are particularly important within a new aquarium where the natural bacteria will take some time to grow to a level that it can play its part in the cycle.

See Figure 2 for a simple illustration of The Nitrogen Cycle in an Aquarium.

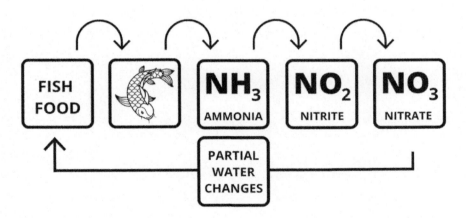

Figure 2: The Nitrogen Cycle in an Aquarium

FLO AQUARIA

DESIRED AND TOLERABLE LEVELS OF AMMONIA, NITRITE AND NITRATE

We measure Ammonia, Nitrite and Nitrate in mg/l (milligrams per litre) or ppm (parts per million), you will often see either or both used at the same time when referring to water testing.

The desired level of Nitrate in a coldwater aquarium is less that 40mg/l ppm.

Where as we should aim for as close as possible to 0mg/l ppm of Ammonia and Nitrite at all times.

In a new aquarium you likely find readings of each but this is understandable as the process of the Nitrogen Cycle can-not begin until these elements exist in some form.

	AMMONIA	NITRITE	NITRATE
TOLERABLE (mg/l ppm)	0-1	0-1	0-40
DESIRED (mg/l ppm)	0	0	0

This is why regular partial water changes are particularly important in a new aquarium and form a vitally important part of ongoing aquarium care.

pH AND THE NITROGEN CYCLE

Lastly, you must also consider the pH of your aquarium water.

pH stands for Potential Hydrogen.

It is the common measure of acidity or alkalinity of a solution, in our case water.

This could be the water you prepare and add to your aquarium or the water that is in your aquarium already, the pH of each will not necessarily be the same.

pH is measured on a scale of 1-14.

Strongly acidic water is pH0 and water with a high measure of alkalinity is pH14.

In the middle of the scale is pH7, a neutral pH (water that is neither too acidic nor alkaline).

The pH of the water in your aquarium will have a large impact on the effectiveness of the Nitrogen Cycle and will directly affect the waters capacity to sustain the bacteria needed for the Nitrogen Cycle to occur.

In very simple terms, a pH lower than 6 can make it difficult for Nitrosomonas to convert Ammonia to Nitrite, if the pH continues to fall even lower still then the Nitrosonomas may stop functioning altogether and the cycle may stop completely.

This would cause a rapid uncontrolled rise in Ammonia (an Ammonia spike) that would kill your fish.

At the other end of the scale when the pH of water is greater than 9, the toxicity of Ammonia in the water increases significantly.

Aim for a neutral pH7-7.5 when keeping goldfish.

Most temperate varieties will desire similar or close to this but check with your local pet store when you begin to expand your collection of fish.

In Chapter 11, WATER TESTING, we will discuss how you can test for Ammonia (NH3), Nitrite (NO2), Nitrate (NO3) and also the pH of your aquarium water.

The GUIDE TO WATER CHANGES in Chapter 12, will take you through the process of managing your partial water changes, step by step, for the first 4 weeks of your new aquarium.

It will help you to manage your Nitrate levels, while the natural bacteria in your aquarium mature and your filters become established.

It will also give you advice on water changes in an established aquarium to help you into the future.

CHAPTER 6

AQUARIUM SAFETY OVERVIEW

This guide is filled with cautionary advice but we feel it is important to stress some points specifically.

The advice is not intended to replace the guidance of any supervising responsible adult or the safety advice and instruction provided with any equipment.

This information is intended as a guide only to supplement the advice of your responsible adult.

Always have an adult supervise when you set up your tank or operate any electrical equipment.

Ensure you have dry hands at all times when operating electrical equipment.

Switch of all power to the aquarium before doing any maintenance tasks or placing your hands or any cleaning items into the aquarium water.

Ask an adult to help you use circuit breakers on all plugs and form drip loops on electrical cables and airlines to ensure that no water can track down to your power source or pump.

Drip loops are formed by ensuring the cable or airline falls lower than the plug or device so that water would drip-off before it reaches the plug or appliance

Make sure your aquarium is positioned on a stable surface and never attempt to move it when full.

Never leave your aquarium uncovered when unattended and be cautious when preparing water that no buckets of water are left unattended.

Wash your hands thoroughly after all maintenance.

Be cautious around your aquarium and take care not to damage the glass or acrylic tank.

Read, follow and keep the manufacturer's instructions for any equipment.

CHAPTER 7

AQUARIUM CHECK LIST

Take time to research and become familiar with all the items on the list.

You will likely be able to purchase most items from your local pet shop or aquarium retailer.

They will be a great source of information and advice as you progress in the hobby and you should find they are happy to provide you with guidance.

Shop around if you can and explore the options available making sure the equipment you buy is suitable for your own needs.

Before you begin you will need:

- Tank & Non slip/ cushioned Tank Mat

- Gravel/ Decorative Stones

- Plants and Decorations

- Filter & Air Pump

- Air Line /Air stone/ Non Return Valve

- Thermometer

- Water Conditioner

- Bucket

- Sieve/ Colander

- Paper Towels/ New Unused Cloths

- Water Test Kit

Once your tank is ready you will also need:

- Small Net

- Fish Food

- Siphon/ Gravel Vacuum/ Algae Scraper

The Equipment you use to maintain your aquarium should be new, or otherwise unused, and should never be used for anything else other than aquarium maintenance.

Household cleaning products, even in the smallest of amounts, could harm your fish and damage your water quality.

Keep your Equipment stored away when not in use and separate from household cleaning items.

CHAPTER 8

FIND THE BEST POSITION FOR

YOUR AQUARIUM

Before you begin following the steps to set up your aquarium you should take time to consider where in your home it will live.

Think about where you want to be able to see your tank from.

Where will you sit to watch your fish in their underwater world?

Will the noise of the pumps or filters cause a disturbance where you have chosen to place your tank?

When full you won't be able to move the tank safely, so you should take time to plan the best position for you and your family.

You will need a flat solid surface such as a solid table or suitable tank stand; that will be able to take the weight of the tank, water, gravel and decorations when the aquarium is full.

1Litre (L) of water weighs 1Killogram (Kg) so if you can see how even a small tank will be very heavy when full.

Make sure your aquarium is away from direct sunlight or radiators/ heaters; this will minimise the chance of water temperature fluctuating or being artificially changed.

Sunlight can also increase Algae growth that will make your water look green and will use up oxygen in the water.

Your electrical supply should be close enough that you can plug in your tanks pump, filter and light, but not too close that there is any danger of water being splashed or dripped onto the electrical sockets or any other nearby electrical equipment.

WATER AND ELECTRICITY ARE VERY DANGEROUS TOGETHER SO ALWAYS EXTRA TAKE CARE.

Be sure you have read the guidance in Chapter 6, AQUARIUM SAFETY OVERVIEW, follow the safety guidance on all equipment and the follow the guidance and advice of your responsible adult.

FLO AQUARIA

CHAPTER 9

SETTING UP YOUR AQUARIUM

The set-up of the aquarium can be shown simply in 10 simple steps;

1. Position/Clean your Tank.
2. Clean/Add your Decorative Stones.
3. Set-up your Filter/ Air Pump.
4. Prepare Water
5. Half fill your Tank.
6. Clean/Add your Decorations.
7. Fill your Tank fully.
8. Power up your Filter/ Air pump.
9. Test Water
10. Safely begin adding Fish.

The following pages go into further detail that explains each step fully.

Don't be worried or overwhelmed, the set up of the aquarium is all part of the fun of beginning fish keeping and you will start to become familiar with the different parts of the tank and get used to it being in your home or bedroom.

You will enjoy it all the more when you finally add fish and they will be much safer, happier and healthier if you don't rush the process.

1) POSITION AND CLEAN YOUR TANK

Now you have found the best position for your aquarium place the empty tank onto a soft anti-slip mat and wipe it down with a clean, damp, cloth to remove any dirt or dust.

The anti-slip mat will protect the base of the tank and the surface it is now resting on.

With the position of your tank decided you can begin to prepare the contents of the aquarium and then start to design your underwater world.

2) CLEAN AND ADD YOUR DECORATIVE STONES

Empty some of your decorative stones/gravel into the colander and wash the stones through with water until the water that runs off them is clear - put these stones into your bucket and repeat with the remaining stones from the packaging until all stones have been cleaned. Once your bucket is full with clean stones you might even want to repeat the whole process again as it can be difficult to get rid of all the dirt and dust the first time around.

When you are happy that your decorative stones are as clean as can be then use a scoop or empty plastic beaker to begin adding the stones to the tank - be careful as even though your tank will be strong, it can still be damaged, so be gentle and don't pour or drop the stones in from any height.

Once you have added all of your decorative stones/gravel, you can move them around to make the stones to the rear of the tank slightly higher than those at the front. This will help to show the decorations and plants you will soon add to the rear of the tank.

These stones make up part of the landscape of your aquarium we call the substrate. Along with looking attractive they will provide a place for beneficial bacteria to live.

Stones can also unfortunately be somewhere that large amounts of waste (fish poo and waste food) can get trapped so make sure you don't add too deep of a layer that will be difficult to clean as time passes.

3) SET-UP YOUR FILTER & AIR PUMP

Set up your filter and air pump following the instructions supplied.

DO NOT TURN ON OR PLUG IN ANY OF THE EQUIPMENT YET.

Often the filter will hang on the back of the tank, sitting on the inside of the glass to one side but the choice on where you place them is yours; think about putting them in a position that you will be able to obstruct (hide) them from being seen when you are looking into the tank later on - a well placed plant or decoration might help with this when they are soon added.

If your air pump is not built in to your filter it will possibly sit outside of the tank and connect to the aquarium using a thin flexible rubber hose known as a airline.

When an air-stone is fitted to the end of this airline (on the tank end) it will break the air up and create lots of small bubbles in your water when turned on.

These bubbles will add oxygen to the water and your fish will breathe this oxygen through their gills.

Always add a non-return valve to the air-line on the part of the hose that is just outside of the tank.

This valve will make sure that water can-not come up the hose and make its way to the air pump.

Use the cable entry holes in your tanks lid to keep cables and hoses safe and well managed but do not plug in or turn on any equipment yet.

See the advice on drip loops in Chapter 6 , AQUARIUM SAFETY OVERVIEW when you later move on to plugging equipment in.

HELPFUL TIP

You should never ever run any of the electrical equipment when the tank doesn't have water inside of it, safely covering the parts of the equipment that are meant to be under the water.

4) PREPARE YOUR WATER

Water from your tap is treated with Chlorine and/or Chloramines to make sure that bacteria can-not live in the water that could make humans ill.

This makes it safe for you to drink and use in your home.

Though it is safe for you to drink tap water containing chlorine/ chloramines the same water will be harmful to your fish.

To rid the water of the chlorine/chloramines you need to add a water conditioner; this will make the water <u>fish safe</u> and in many cases add beneficial bacteria that will help to start good bacteria growing in your filters and tank water.

To make this process easier prepare your water in a bucket.

Follow the instructions on your chosen water conditioner carefully. Be as careful as possible when measuring out your water conditioner and try to use a bucket with measurements on the inside for the water.

If you don't have a bucket with measurements on you could use a measuring jug and make a note as you add each jug of water to the bucket so you have some idea of the amount of water you are mixing the water conditioner into.

Always stir the water fully once you have added the water conditioner.

Don't worry if your bucket will only fill the tank partly, we only want to fill it half full to start with and you can make as many separate buckets of fish safe water as needed by repeating this process.

The most important part of this step is ensuring you use the right amount of conditioner to the amount of water in your bucket each time.

5) HALF FILL YOUR TANK

Using the water you have prepared, carefully fill the tank so it is around half full, this will make it easier for you to decorate your aquarium in the next step.

So you don't disturb the stones you have already added you should place a small bowl or plate in the bottom of your tank and gently pour the water on to this to stop the water splashing directly in to the stones.

The bowl/ plate can be removed when you have finished and your effort to make things look good so far will not be wasted.

6) ADD YOUR DECORATIONS

Wash all decorations thoroughly and make sure you only use items intended for use in an aquarium.

Add any large pebbles, plants and decorations and move them around until you are happy with the layout of the tank. When you are happy you can gentle cover the base of each item below the level of your decorative stones and this will make for a neater more natural appearance

Spread tall items around the back of the tank and smaller ones to the front, to create depth to your design and make it easier for you to watch your fish.

Make sure you still have lots of space for your fish to swim.

HELPFUL TIP

Because this is your first tank we recommend only using decorations you have purchased that are specifically designed to be used in a fish tank.

Some natural items such as wood and stone will change the water quality and can make it harder to manage or completely unsafe for fish to live in.

Items you haven't bought as fish safe will always need special preparation before use underwater.

Apart from the danger from hidden bacteria and bugs, some types of wood for example can change the colour of your water and some types of stone can dissolve slowly changing the chemical balance of your water and harming your fish.

7) FINISH FILLING YOUR TANK

Following the method discussed previously prepare enough water to fill the rest of your tank.

Fill the tank to the ensure all filtration equipment is fully submerged or submerged to the water fill line on the equipment if relevant.

Usually you will want the water to be filled up to around 1inch (2.5cm) below the trim around the top of the tank, this is because even with a lid on the tank, water will still splash as bubbles from your aeration reach the water's surface.

The maximum height that you fill the tank to is called THE WATER LINE.

8) POWER UP YOUR EQUIPMENT

Wipe up any splashes of water from the earlier steps of this guide, store away any equipment you have used and tidy the area around your tank.

Dry your hands thoroughly and then carefully follow the instructions on your filter, pump, and light to switch each on.

The water conditioner you added earlier should mean your water is now safe for fish to be added.

It is however a good idea to resist the temptation to add fish straight away, and allow your aquarium to run without fish for 24-48 hours to make sure all of your equipment is working properly.

Though unlikely this will also give you time to see if any leaks occur in your tank.

9) TEST YOUR WATER

You will need to test your water regularly following the so you know that it is as safe as possible for your fish.

From the results of these water tests you will be able to see if you have to take any action to correct it.

To start with it is useful to take your first reading before you progress to adding fish, this will give you a base reading to compare as you progress and also allow you to check the pH of your water.

See Chapter 11, WATER TESTING.

Begin a record of your water test results in Chapter 16.

10) ADD JUST A FEW FISH

Having waited for 24hours and tested your water you can now begin your collection of fish by adding just 1 or 2 small fish to your aquarium following the guidance on the next page.

Remember, because your tank is new you will only have small amounts of the good beneficial bacteria in your filter

You need to let the good beneficial bacteria grow (become established) to a level that the beneficial bacteria can cope with a larger amount of waste before you add a larger number of fish.

HOW TO ADD FISH SAFELY

Fish are very sensitive to changes in the water they are in.

Following this guidance will help them to acclimatise to your aquariums water temperature and conditions; this will avoid stressing them or causing them harm.

1) Turn off your aquarium lights and lower the light in the room your aquarium is in.

2) Float the bag containing the new fish in your tank for around 15-20 minutes. Keep the bag tied closed at this time and this will allow the water in the bag to reach a temperature closer to that of the water in your tank.

3) Open the bag and roll the sides down a little. This will make an air pocket that helps the bag to float open in your water.

4) Add a little water from your tank to the bag (around half a cup) then repeat this step every 5minutes until the bag is full.

5) When full remove half of the water from the bag to waste (Do not tip this water into your tank).Repeat the half cup fill up method from Step 4 every 5minutes until the bag is full again.

6) Now the bag is full for a second time you can gently transfer the fish from the bag into the aquarium using a small care net.

7) Remove the bag full of water and empty as waste water (again do not tip this water into your tank).

Note the time you added the new fish and watch it carefully over the next 24 hours; make notes in this book on its behaviour until you are sure it is settled.

A NOTE ON ADDING MORE FISH TO YOUR AQUARIUM

Read and understand THE NITROGEN CYCLE EXPLAINED; WATER TESTING and the GUIDE TO WATER CHANGES first, before you consider adding more fish to your aquarium.

GENERAL NOTES

Your tanks Filter and Air Pump should run for 24 hours a day and only ever be switched off during maintenance.

Your tanks lighting should be on for around 8 hours each day or roughly follow daylight hours.

Feed your fish as per the guidance on the next page, once per day at first and then as per the instruction on your chosen food when the tank is mature. At times it may be necessary to adjust the feeding routine to help with managing water quality.

FLO AQUARIA

CHAPTER 10

THE FIRST WEEKS OF YOUR

NEW AQUARIUM

Your water may turn cloudy in the days following you adding your first fish.

This will most likely be as a result of a bacteria bloom and is a sign that the bacteria your filters need to function is beginning to grow - don't be worried this is normal and it should clear within a few days.

Your fish may be quite shy at this time and will likely make use of the decorations you have added to hide away from you or one another.

Feed your fish sparingly until your water readings are stable and only give them what they can eat within about 2 minutes.

Avoid food being wasted as uneaten food will rot in the water and add to the increase in Ammonia along with making your water cloudy.

If you are overfeeding you will see waste food on the stones in the bottom of the tank, this is a sign you should reduce the amount of food you are adding each time.

Other signs include a strong odour when you remove your tank lid and foaming on the surface of the water.

After 14 days or so you may also start to see Algae forming on the glass of your aquarium, follow the guidance in Chapter 13, to resolve and manage this.

CHAPTER 11

WATER TESTING

As we have previously discussed, we need to regularly test our aquarium water.

Testing can be done in one of two ways at this beginner level:

1) Test Strips

2) Test Kits

At an advanced level you can purchase expensive electronic testing equipment but as this is a beginner's guide we will only discuss the two options above.

Test Strips

Based on experience, we recommend that the use of water test strips should be avoided as the results you get are often very difficult to read and understand.

You may not get the level of information you require from this method of testing and you will almost certainly find you need to purchase a full test kit at some stage in the future.

Test Kits

Simple test kits can be purchased at a price affordable to all hobbyists.

The basic water test kits containing water test tubes, chemical agents and easy to read charts should suffice for you at a beginner level and perhaps far beyond.

The specific instructions for use will be different with each kit so we can-not advise you exactly on this, but can give you a general idea of the method and confirm that this is the type of water test kit we recommend.

Usually you will take a measured sample of water from your aquarium with a syringe and this will be placed into a test-tube, you will add one or several chemicals to this test tube in a specific order and then wait for a designated amount of time to pass.

When ready you will compare the colour of the water with a chart that is provided, and this will give you your reading.

These kits make the process very straightforward and quite apart from the welfare of your fish you should consider a water test kit a great investment against the value of your fish and a fun part of your hobby.

Be organised when you test water, have a pen or pencil to hand, and use a timer to help you.

Always record your results using the TEST, CHANGE, CHECK log sheets in Chapter 16.

CHAPTER 12

GUIDE TO WATER CHANGES

In previous chapters we have talked about the Nitrogen Cycle in your Aquarium, the desired levels of Ammonia, Nitrite and Nitrate and how to perform water testing.

Now your aquarium is set-up and is home to your few starter fish, you need to begin managing the hidden waste in the water, and help support the aquarium towards it managing Ammonia, Nitrite and Nitrate itself.

This chapter will outline the steps you can take to manage the levels of each with regular partial water changes.

From the end of Week 1 onwards you will begin a process of water testing and changes.

Usually you will test and then perform a partial water change every week for the first 4 weeks or until your Nitrate readings begin to fall.

During weeks 1-4 if a water change is needed then take care not to disturb the gravel in the base of your aquarium, don't vacuum the gravel yet, just remove water.

If you are worried about a build-up of debris then remove the excess with your small net.

Water can easily be removed using a siphon kit many of which will come with a gravel vacuum attachment that can be used later on in your fish keeping journey.

Siphon the water into your bucket; if you know the volume of your aquarium and your bucket has some measurements noted on it, you will find the process much easier and can be more accurate with the amount of water you remove - See Chapter 14 CALCULATE THE VOLUME OF YOUR AQUARIUM and Chapter 15 WATER CHANGE % IN LITRES FOR YOUR AQUARIUM.

After this 4 week period, once your Nitrate levels fall and stabilise you will be able to reduce your partial water changes to a fortnightly change and then in time perhaps even a monthly change.

Regardless of how long your aquarium has been set up and how mature your filters, you should always maintain the weekly water tests to monitor the water parameters.

Follow the guidance in the week by week charts and look for the Nitrate levels falling as the week's progress.

DAYS 1-6

<u>You should not change any water during the first week</u> of the few fish being added, this will allow natural bacteria to begin to grow.

Because you have only added just a few fish and you are not overfeeding, the rise in your AMMONIA, NITRITE AND NITRATE should rise as gently as possible this week.

This gentle rise should be manageable with water changes, beginning at day 7, if necessary.

(See Week 1 table for guidance).

Many products exist to control Ammonia, Nitrite and Nitrate but you should avoid adding anything to the water that will ultimately hinder the natural nitrogen cycle.

Let nature take its course and help it along with these water changes.

Common Mistakes

One of the most common mistakes made at this stage is overfeeding your fish and creating a huge spike in Ammonia that your aquarium will not have the natural bacteria to handle.

You will notice we mention overfeeding a lot in the following pages and this is not just a coincidence or poor editing on our part, over-feeding can create a very real hazard in your aquarium at any time but in particular when it is new and your filter have yet to mature.

At this stage in your fish keeping journey your Fish are far more likely to come to harm from over-feeding, rather than under-feeding, so take extra care to avoid over-feeding and the water care problems it will create.

WEEK 1
7 DAYS AFTER THE INTRODUCTION OF FISH

TEST YOUR WATER FOR NITRATE
ARE YOUR RESULTS ABOVE 40ppm?

NO | THIS IS GREAT, A POSITIVE START, KEEP GOING AS YOU ARE AND DO NOT PERFORM A WATER CHANGE THIS WEEK.

YES | DONT WORRY THIS IS COMMON WITH A NEW AQUARIUM BUT YOU DO NEED TO TAKE ACTION TO CONTROL THE RISE IN NITRATE. PERFORM A 30% WATER CHANGE AND MAKE SURE NOT TO OVERFEED DURING THE FOLLOWING WEEK.

ALWAYS RECORD ANY TEST RESULTS AND MAKE A NOTE OF ANYTHING YOU HAVE DONE IN YOUR LOGBOOK

WEEK 2

14 DAYS AFTER THE INTRODUCTION OF FISH

TEST YOUR WATER FOR NITRATE
ARE YOUR RESULTS ABOVE 40ppm?

NO | THINGS APPEAR TO BE GOING WELL, KEEP GOING AS YOU ARE AND DO NOT PERFORM A WATER CHANGE THIS WEEK.

YES | DONT WORRY THIS IS COMMON WITH A NEW AQUARIUM BUT YOU DO NEED TO TAKE ACTION TO CONTROL THE RISE IN NITRATE.

PERFORM A 50% WATER CHANGE AND MAKE SURE NOT TO OVERFEED DURING THE FOLLOWING WEEK.

ALWAYS RECORD ANY TEST RESULTS AND MAKE A NOTE OF ANYTHING YOU HAVE DONE IN YOUR LOGBOOK

WEEK 3

21 DAYS AFTER THE INTRODUCTION OF FISH

TEST YOUR WATER FOR NITRATE
ARE YOUR RESULTS HIGHER THAN WEEK 2?

NO		EXCELLENT, NITRATES ARE FALLING, KEEP GOING AS YOU ARE AND DO NOT PERFORM A WATER CHANGE THIS WEEK.

YES		YOUR AQUARIUM MAY BE OVERSTOCKED/ UNDERSIZED THEREFORE IT MAY NEED A LITTLE MORE ONGOING MAINTAINANCE TO KEEP IT HEALTHY. UNDERTAKE A 50% WATER CHANGE TODAY, TEST AND REPEAT THE 50% CHANGE EVERY 4 DAYS UNTIL THE NITRATE IS BELOW 40ppm AND FALLING.

ALWAYS RECORD ANY TEST RESULTS AND MAKE A NOTE OF ANYTHING YOU HAVE DONE IN YOUR LOGBOOK

WEEK 4
28 DAYS AFTER THE INTRODUCTION OF FISH

TEST YOUR WATER FOR NITRATE
ARE YOUR RESULTS HIGHER THAN WEEK 3?

NO	BRILLIANT, YOU NOW HAVE TWO OPTIONS BASED ON YOUR NITRATE TEST RESULTS OVER PREVIOUS WEEKS. SEE THE NEXT PAGE FOR GUIDANCE.
YES	REDUCE FEEDING TO EVERY OTHER DAY CONTINUE TO MAKE 50% WATER CHANGES EVERY 4 DAYS UNTIL NITRATE LEVELS FALL AND STABILISE. CONSIDER ADDITIONAL FILTRATION (WITH A LARGER AMOUNT OF FILTER MEDIA), PURCHASING A LARGER AQUARIUM OR REDUCING FISH NUMBERS.

ALWAYS RECORD ANY TEST RESULTS AND MAKE A NOTE OF ANYTHING YOU HAVE DONE IN YOUR LOGBOOK

YOUR WEEK 4 RESULTS WERE LOWER THAN WEEK 3, BUT WERE YOUR WEEK 3 RESULTS ALREADY BELOW 40ppm?

NO |

IF YOU ARE NOW BELOW 40ppm BUT THIS HAS HAPPENED ONLY RECENTLY YOU MAY BENEFIT FROM A FURTHER SMALL WATER CHANGE THIS WEEK BEFORE MOVING TO A REDUCED WATER CHANGE ROUTINE.

PERFORM A 20% CHANGE AND TEST AGAIN IN 7 DAYS, IF YOUR RESULTS ARE STILL STABLE THEN WAIT A FURTHER 7 DAYS BEFORE TESTING AGAIN.

IF LEVELS ARE CONSISTENTLY STABLE YOU CAN PERFORM A 30-40% CHANGE MONTHLY.

YES |

YOUR RESULTS HAVE BEEN IN THE TOLERABLE RANGE FOR SOME TIME. YOU SEEM TO HAVE A EASY TO MAINTAIN AQUARIUM.

WE SUGGEST WEEKLY TESTING AND A 15% MONTHLY WATER CHANGE

WEEK 5 ONWARD

As the beneficial bacteria continue to grow and the filters continue to mature the readings you get should begin to level out and become more controlled.

With mature aquarium filters containing lots of beneficial bacteria, providing your tank is not overstocked and your filter is adequate your Ammonia and Nitrite levels should manage themselves.

The water changes at this time will then mainly serve to manage the Nitrate levels.

When the filters reach this stage we call them established and the aquarium is considered to be cycled and mature.

Rather than a weekly change, with established filters you should only need to perform a routine partial change monthly.

Be sure to still test regularly and carry out a partial change if the readings are of any concern.

BUT WHEN CAN I ADD MORE FISH?

When you have established filters and regular consistent water readings you can begin to slowly add more fish to your tank making sure your water readings over the coming weeks continue to stay controlled.

CHAPTER 13

ROUTINE MAINTENANCE

FOR A MATURE AQUARIUM

During your routine water change you should remove algae from the aquarium glass using a soft sponge or glass cloth and algae scraper, following this gently vacuum the gravel using your gravel vacuum while you are siphoning water from the Aquarium.

Each month you should replace the carbon pads in your aquarium filter; this can be done with your monthly water change.

On a monthly basis you should also remove the mechanical filter pads/sponges from your filter and rinse them with water from your aquarium to remove excess debris.

Try to do this in-between the weeks that you perform your water change so that you are not making two big changes to the aquariums bacteria content at the same time.

Add a small amount of water from your aquarium to your bucket, place the filter pads/sponges in the water.

Gently shake of the excess debris before replacing the filter pads/ sponges back in the filter.

Discard this water and do not return it to your aquarium.

ESSENTIAL TIP

Never use Tap Water to rinse your filter pads/ sponges as this will kill the bacteria that they contain and damage the delicate balance of good bacteria in your aquarium.

FLO AQUARIA

CHAPTER 14

CALCULATE AND RECORD YOUR AQUARIUM VOLUME

The amount of water in your aquarium is known as its volume.

The volume of your aquarium is important to know for lots of reasons.

You can use the volume to work out how many fish can live happily in your tank, how much water you need to change when needed, and even how much medicine to add to your water if you ever need to treat your fish for an illness.

You might have bought a certain size of tank but the volume of water you have when you fill it to the height you want it to be, might be slightly different from the noted volume.

To work out the volume of your aquarium you will need to take some measurements, you can do this with a ruler or ask an adult to help you with a tape measure.

Measure the water from one side to the other to find how long it is (length). Measure from front to back to find how wide it is (width) and measure from top to bottom to find how high it is (height) - write your measurements on page 93 and we will use them to work out your volume.

Remember, you want to measure the amount of water you have and not the size of your tank.

Be careful to only measure up to the waterline in your aquarium.

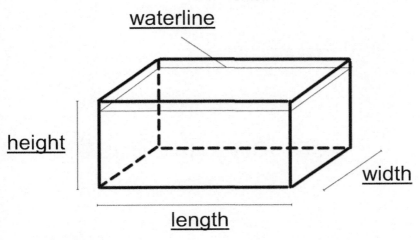

HELPFUL TIP

Use a small piece of tape to mark the waterline in your aquarium.

The waterline should be around 2.5cm from the top of your tank.

Use this as a guide so that each time complete a partial water change and you top up the water, you can always get it back to the same height.

This will mean you always have the same volume of water when your aquarium is full to the waterline.

MY AQUARIUM MEASURES

length _____ cm long (its length)

width _____ cm wide (its width)

height _____ cm high (its height)

On the next page you can add these figures to a calculation and ask an adult to help you work out the sum.

From this you will find the volume of your tank in centimetres cubed (cm^3).

<u>MY AQUARIUM VOLUME IN cm^3</u>

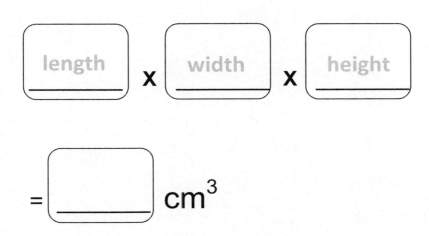

length X width X height

= _____ cm^3

Now you know how many cm^3 you have in your tank, you can do another sum to work out how many Litres (L), you have in your tank.

<u>MY AQUARIUM VOLUME IN LITRES (L)</u>

$1cm^3$ is equal to 0.001 L

And from this we know that 1000cm3 is equal to 1 L

If you add the cm^3 figure from your first calculation to the sum below and work out the answer, you will know how many Litres are in your tank.

 cm3 X 0.001

= _____ L

As the volume of fish tanks are also commonly measured in Gallons (G).

MY AQUARIUM VOLUME IN GALLONS (G)

Using the figure we have calculated for the volume in Litres you can now also now work out the amount of water in your tank in Gallons.

1Litre is equal to 0.22 G

If you add the L figure from the previous calculation to the sum below, and work out the answer, you will know how many Gallons are in your tank.

_____ L x 0.22

= _____ G

CHAPTER 15

WATER CHANGE % IN LITRES

FOR YOUR AQUARIUM

Add your tank Volume in Litres below and divide it by 100 to work out what 1% of your tanks volume is.

You can then multiply this figure to find your water change percentages in Litres for the various common water change percentages you might need.

Overall Volume in Litres/ 100 = 1%

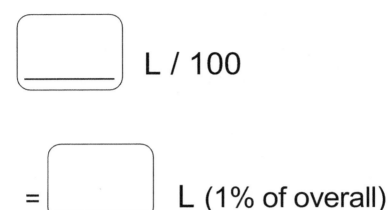

L / 100

= [   ] L (1% of overall)

If you multiply this 1% figure by the percentages on the following pages you can find the common amounts of water you might need to remove and replace when you carry-out your partial water changes.

Remember these will only be accurate if your tank is full to the waterline to begin with.

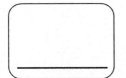 L (1% of overall)

X 15 = [_____] L

YOUR 15% CHANGE

X 20 = [_____] L

YOUR 20% CHANGE

X 30 = [_____] L

YOUR 30% CHANGE

X 40 = [_____] L

YOUR 40% CHANGE

X 50 = [_____] L

YOUR 50% CHANGE

CHAPTER 16

RECORD SHEETS

AND JOURNAL PAGES

12 Months of record keeping sheets

and journal pages

for you to complete and keep.

TEST/ CHANGE / CHECK

/ /	AM PM	°C	DAYS SINCE LAST TEST

TEST

RESULT ☺ ☹

		☺ ☹
NH₃ AMMONIA	ppm	☺ ☐ ☹ ☐
NO₂ NITRITE	ppm	☺ ☐ ☹ ☐
NO₃ NITRATE	ppm	☺ ☐ ☹ ☐
pH	pH	☺ ☐ ☹ ☐

CHECK

FILTERS

CHECKED ☐	CLEANED ☐	**OR**	CHANGED ☐

PUMP	CHECKED ☐
AIRLINE	CHECKED ☐
LIGHTING	CHECKED ☐

CHANGE   NOTE WATER CHANGED AFTER TEST AS A PERCENTAGE   %

WATER TEST/ CHANGE NOTES

FISH COUNT
#

WEEK BEGINNING: / /	FEED TIMES

MONDAY *ADD DAILY NOTES AND OBSERVATIONS*

HIDING	**FISH BEHAVIOUR**	ACTIVE
1	2	3	4	5

AM
___
PM

TUESDAY

HIDING	**FISH BEHAVIOUR**	ACTIVE
1	2	3	4	5

AM
___
PM

WEDNESDAY

HIDING	**FISH BEHAVIOUR**	ACTIVE
1	2	3	4	5

AM
___
PM

THURSDAY

HIDING	**FISH BEHAVIOUR**	ACTIVE
1	2	3	4	5

AM
___
PM

FRIDAY

HIDING	**FISH BEHAVIOUR**	ACTIVE
1	2	3	4	5

AM
___
PM

SATURDAY

HIDING	**FISH BEHAVIOUR**	ACTIVE
1	2	3	4	5

AM
___
PM

SUNDAY

HIDING	**FISH BEHAVIOUR**	ACTIVE
1	2	3	4	5

AM
___
PM

TEST/ CHANGE / CHECK

| / / | | AM PM | °C | DAYS SINCE LAST TEST | |

TEST

RESULT 🙂 🙁

NH₃ AMMONIA		ppm	🙂 ☐	🙁 ☐
NO₂ NITRITE		ppm	🙂 ☐	🙁 ☐
NO₃ NITRATE		ppm	🙂 ☐	🙁 ☐
pH		pH	🙂 ☐	🙁 ☐

CHECK

FILTERS

| CHECKED ☐ | CLEANED ☐ | **OR** | CHANGED ☐ |

PUMP	CHECKED ☐
AIRLINE	CHECKED ☐
LIGHTING	CHECKED ☐

CHANGE   NOTE WATER CHANGED AFTER TEST AS A PERCENTAGE   %

WATER TEST/ CHANGE NOTES

FISH COUNT
#

WEEK BEGINNING: /   /

MONDAY *ADD DAILY NOTES AND OBSERVATIONS*

HIDING	FISH BEHAVIOUR			ACTIVE
1	2	3	4	5

AM
___
PM

TUESDAY

HIDING	FISH BEHAVIOUR			ACTIVE
1	2	3	4	5

AM
___
PM

WEDNESDAY

HIDING	FISH BEHAVIOUR			ACTIVE
1	2	3	4	5

AM
___
PM

THURSDAY

HIDING	FISH BEHAVIOUR			ACTIVE
1	2	3	4	5

AM
___
PM

FRIDAY

HIDING	FISH BEHAVIOUR			ACTIVE
1	2	3	4	5

AM
___
PM

SATURDAY

HIDING	FISH BEHAVIOUR			ACTIVE
1	2	3	4	5

AM
___
PM

SUNDAY

HIDING	FISH BEHAVIOUR			ACTIVE
1	2	3	4	5

AM
___
PM

TEST/ CHANGE / CHECK

| / / | | AM / PM | | °C | | DAYS SINCE LAST TEST | |

TEST

RESULT ☺ ☹

				☺ ☐	☹ ☐
NH₃ AMMONIA		ppm		☺ ☐	☹ ☐
NO₂ NITRITE		ppm		☺ ☐	☹ ☐
NO₃ NITRATE		ppm		☺ ☐	☹ ☐
pH		pH		☺ ☐	☹ ☐

CHECK

FILTERS

| CHECKED ☐ | CLEANED ☐ | OR | CHANGED ☐ |

PUMP	CHECKED ☐
AIRLINE	CHECKED ☐
LIGHTING	CHECKED ☐

CHANGE

NOTE WATER CHANGED AFTER TEST AS A PERCENTAGE

%

WATER TEST/ CHANGE NOTES

FISH COUNT

#

WEEK BEGINNING: / /	FEED TIMES

MONDAY *ADD DAILY NOTES AND OBSERVATIONS*

HIDING **FISH BEHAVIOUR** ACTIVE
| 1 | 2 | 3 | 4 | 5 |

AM
—
PM

TUESDAY

HIDING **FISH BEHAVIOUR** ACTIVE
| 1 | 2 | 3 | 4 | 5 |

AM
—
PM

WEDNESDAY

HIDING **FISH BEHAVIOUR** ACTIVE
| 1 | 2 | 3 | 4 | 5 |

AM
—
PM

THURSDAY

HIDING **FISH BEHAVIOUR** ACTIVE
| 1 | 2 | 3 | 4 | 5 |

AM
—
PM

FRIDAY

HIDING **FISH BEHAVIOUR** ACTIVE
| 1 | 2 | 3 | 4 | 5 |

AM
—
PM

SATURDAY

HIDING **FISH BEHAVIOUR** ACTIVE
| 1 | 2 | 3 | 4 | 5 |

AM
—
PM

SUNDAY

HIDING **FISH BEHAVIOUR** ACTIVE
| 1 | 2 | 3 | 4 | 5 |

AM
—
PM

TEST/ CHANGE / CHECK

| / / | AM PM | °C | DAYS SINCE LAST TEST | |

TEST

RESULT ☺ ☹

NH₃ AMMONIA		ppm	☺ ☐	☹ ☐
NO₂ NITRITE		ppm	☺ ☐	☹ ☐
NO₃ NITRATE		ppm	☺ ☐	☹ ☐
pH		pH	☺ ☐	☹ ☐

CHECK

FILTERS

| CHECKED ☐ | CLEANED ☐ | OR | CHANGED ☐ |

PUMP	CHECKED ☐
AIRLINE	CHECKED ☐
LIGHTING	CHECKED ☐

CHANGE

NOTE WATER CHANGED AFTER TEST AS A PERCENTAGE

%

WATER TEST/ CHANGE NOTES

FISH COUNT

#

WEEK BEGINNING: /   /

MONDAY *ADD DAILY NOTES AND OBSERVATIONS*

HIDING	FISH BEHAVIOUR			ACTIVE
1	2	3	4	5

AM
___
PM

TUESDAY

HIDING	FISH BEHAVIOUR			ACTIVE
1	2	3	4	5

AM
___
PM

WEDNESDAY

HIDING	FISH BEHAVIOUR			ACTIVE
1	2	3	4	5

AM
___
PM

THURSDAY

HIDING	FISH BEHAVIOUR			ACTIVE
1	2	3	4	5

AM
___
PM

FRIDAY

HIDING	FISH BEHAVIOUR			ACTIVE
1	2	3	4	5

AM
___
PM

SATURDAY

HIDING	FISH BEHAVIOUR			ACTIVE
1	2	3	4	5

AM
___
PM

SUNDAY

HIDING	FISH BEHAVIOUR			ACTIVE
1	2	3	4	5

AM
___
PM

TEST/ CHANGE / CHECK

/ /	AM PM	°C	DAYS SINCE LAST TEST

TEST

RESULT   ☺ ☹

NH₃ AMMONIA	ppm	☺ ☐ ☹ ☐
NO₂ NITRITE	ppm	☺ ☐ ☹ ☐
NO₃ NITRATE	ppm	☺ ☐ ☹ ☐
pH	pH	☺ ☐ ☹ ☐

CHECK

FILTERS

CHECKED ☐	CLEANED ☐	OR	CHANGED ☐

PUMP	CHECKED ☐
AIRLINE	CHECKED ☐
LIGHTING	CHECKED ☐

CHANGE   NOTE WATER CHANGED AFTER TEST AS A PERCENTAGE   %

WATER TEST/ CHANGE NOTES

	FISH COUNT #

WEEK BEGINNING: / /

MONDAY *ADD DAILY NOTES AND OBSERVATIONS*

HIDING **FISH BEHAVIOUR** ACTIVE
| 1 | 2 | 3 | 4 | 5 |

AM
___
PM

TUESDAY

HIDING **FISH BEHAVIOUR** ACTIVE
| 1 | 2 | 3 | 4 | 5 |

AM
___
PM

WEDNESDAY

HIDING **FISH BEHAVIOUR** ACTIVE
| 1 | 2 | 3 | 4 | 5 |

AM
___
PM

THURSDAY

HIDING **FISH BEHAVIOUR** ACTIVE
| 1 | 2 | 3 | 4 | 5 |

AM
___
PM

FRIDAY

HIDING **FISH BEHAVIOUR** ACTIVE
| 1 | 2 | 3 | 4 | 5 |

AM
___
PM

SATURDAY

HIDING **FISH BEHAVIOUR** ACTIVE
| 1 | 2 | 3 | 4 | 5 |

AM
___
PM

SUNDAY

HIDING **FISH BEHAVIOUR** ACTIVE
| 1 | 2 | 3 | 4 | 5 |

AM
___
PM

TEST/ CHANGE / CHECK

| / / | AM PM | °C | DAYS SINCE LAST TEST |

TEST

| RESULT | 🙂 ☹️ |

NH₃ AMMONIA		ppm	🙂 ☹️ ☐ ☐
NO₂ NITRITE		ppm	🙂 ☹️ ☐ ☐
NO₃ NITRATE		ppm	🙂 ☹️ ☐ ☐
pH		pH	🙂 ☹️ ☐ ☐

CHECK

FILTERS

| CHECKED ☐ | CLEANED ☐ | OR | CHANGED ☐ |

PUMP	CHECKED ☐
AIRLINE	CHECKED ☐
LIGHTING	CHECKED ☐

CHANGE

NOTE WATER CHANGED AFTER TEST AS A PERCENTAGE

%

WATER TEST/ CHANGE NOTES

FISH COUNT

#

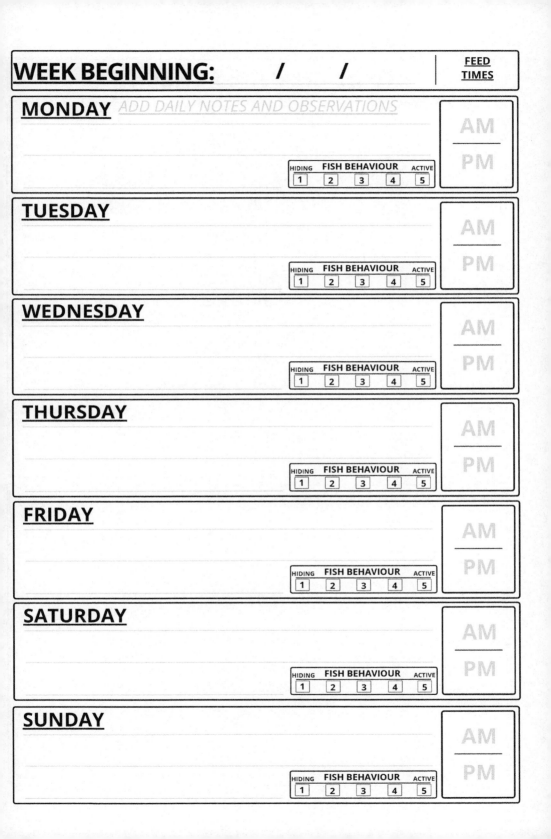

| **WEEK BEGINNING:** / / | **FEED TIMES** |

MONDAY *ADD DAILY NOTES AND OBSERVATIONS*

| HIDING | **FISH BEHAVIOUR** | ACTIVE |
| 1 | 2 | 3 | 4 | 5 |

AM
___
PM

TUESDAY

| HIDING | **FISH BEHAVIOUR** | ACTIVE |
| 1 | 2 | 3 | 4 | 5 |

AM
___
PM

WEDNESDAY

| HIDING | **FISH BEHAVIOUR** | ACTIVE |
| 1 | 2 | 3 | 4 | 5 |

AM
___
PM

THURSDAY

| HIDING | **FISH BEHAVIOUR** | ACTIVE |
| 1 | 2 | 3 | 4 | 5 |

AM
___
PM

FRIDAY

| HIDING | **FISH BEHAVIOUR** | ACTIVE |
| 1 | 2 | 3 | 4 | 5 |

AM
___
PM

SATURDAY

| HIDING | **FISH BEHAVIOUR** | ACTIVE |
| 1 | 2 | 3 | 4 | 5 |

AM
___
PM

SUNDAY

| HIDING | **FISH BEHAVIOUR** | ACTIVE |
| 1 | 2 | 3 | 4 | 5 |

AM
___
PM

TEST/ CHANGE / CHECK

/ /	AM PM	°C	DAYS SINCE LAST TEST	

TEST

RESULT ☺ ☹

NH₃ AMMONIA		ppm	☺ ☹ ☐ ☐
NO₂ NITRITE		ppm	☺ ☹ ☐ ☐
NO₃ NITRATE		ppm	☺ ☹ ☐ ☐
pH		pH	☺ ☹ ☐ ☐

CHECK

FILTERS

CHECKED ☐	CLEANED ☐	OR	CHANGED ☐

PUMP	CHECKED ☐
AIRLINE	CHECKED ☐
LIGHTING	CHECKED ☐

CHANGE NOTE WATER CHANGED AFTER TEST AS A PERCENTAGE %

WATER TEST/ CHANGE NOTES

FISH COUNT

#

WEEK BEGINNING: /   /

FEED TIMES

MONDAY   *ADD DAILY NOTES AND OBSERVATIONS*

HIDING   **FISH BEHAVIOUR**   ACTIVE
| 1 | 2 | 3 | 4 | 5 |

AM
___
PM

TUESDAY

HIDING   **FISH BEHAVIOUR**   ACTIVE
| 1 | 2 | 3 | 4 | 5 |

AM
___
PM

WEDNESDAY

HIDING   **FISH BEHAVIOUR**   ACTIVE
| 1 | 2 | 3 | 4 | 5 |

AM
___
PM

THURSDAY

HIDING   **FISH BEHAVIOUR**   ACTIVE
| 1 | 2 | 3 | 4 | 5 |

AM
___
PM

FRIDAY

HIDING   **FISH BEHAVIOUR**   ACTIVE
| 1 | 2 | 3 | 4 | 5 |

AM
___
PM

SATURDAY

HIDING   **FISH BEHAVIOUR**   ACTIVE
| 1 | 2 | 3 | 4 | 5 |

AM
___
PM

SUNDAY

HIDING   **FISH BEHAVIOUR**   ACTIVE
| 1 | 2 | 3 | 4 | 5 |

AM
___
PM

TEST/ CHANGE / CHECK

/ /	AM PM	°C	DAYS SINCE LAST TEST

TEST

RESULT	☺ ☹

NH₃ AMMONIA	ppm	☺ ☐ ☹ ☐
NO₂ NITRITE	ppm	☺ ☐ ☹ ☐
NO₃ NITRATE	ppm	☺ ☐ ☹ ☐
pH	pH	☺ ☐ ☹ ☐

CHECK

FILTERS

CHECKED ☐	CLEANED ☐	OR	CHANGED ☐

PUMP	CHECKED ☐
AIRLINE	CHECKED ☐
LIGHTING	CHECKED ☐

CHANGE

NOTE WATER CHANGED AFTER TEST AS A PERCENTAGE

%

WATER TEST/ CHANGE NOTES

FISH COUNT

#

WEEK BEGINNING: / /	FEED TIMES

MONDAY *ADD DAILY NOTES AND OBSERVATIONS*

HIDING	**FISH BEHAVIOUR**			ACTIVE
1	2	3	4	5

AM
___
PM

TUESDAY

HIDING	**FISH BEHAVIOUR**			ACTIVE
1	2	3	4	5

AM
___
PM

WEDNESDAY

HIDING	**FISH BEHAVIOUR**			ACTIVE
1	2	3	4	5

AM
___
PM

THURSDAY

HIDING	**FISH BEHAVIOUR**			ACTIVE
1	2	3	4	5

AM
___
PM

FRIDAY

HIDING	**FISH BEHAVIOUR**			ACTIVE
1	2	3	4	5

AM
___
PM

SATURDAY

HIDING	**FISH BEHAVIOUR**			ACTIVE
1	2	3	4	5

AM
___
PM

SUNDAY

HIDING	**FISH BEHAVIOUR**			ACTIVE
1	2	3	4	5

AM
___
PM

TEST/ CHANGE / CHECK

/ /		AM PM		°C	DAYS SINCE LAST TEST

TEST

RESULT ☺ ☹

NH₃ AMMONIA	_____ ppm	☺ ☐ ☹ ☐
NO₂ NITRITE	_____ ppm	☺ ☐ ☹ ☐
NO₃ NITRATE	_____ ppm	☺ ☐ ☹ ☐
pH	_____ pH	☺ ☐ ☹ ☐

CHECK

FILTERS

| CHECKED ☐ | CLEANED ☐ | **OR** | CHANGED ☐ |

PUMP	CHECKED ☐
AIRLINE	CHECKED ☐
LIGHTING	CHECKED ☐

CHANGE   NOTE WATER CHANGED AFTER TEST AS A PERCENTAGE   [%]

WATER TEST/ CHANGE NOTES

FISH COUNT
#

WEEK BEGINNING: / /	FEED TIMES

MONDAY *ADD DAILY NOTES AND OBSERVATIONS*

HIDING	**FISH BEHAVIOUR**	ACTIVE
1	2	3	4	5

AM
___
PM

TUESDAY

HIDING	**FISH BEHAVIOUR**	ACTIVE
1	2	3	4	5

AM
___
PM

WEDNESDAY

HIDING	**FISH BEHAVIOUR**	ACTIVE
1	2	3	4	5

AM
___
PM

THURSDAY

HIDING	**FISH BEHAVIOUR**	ACTIVE
1	2	3	4	5

AM
___
PM

FRIDAY

HIDING	**FISH BEHAVIOUR**	ACTIVE
1	2	3	4	5

AM
___
PM

SATURDAY

HIDING	**FISH BEHAVIOUR**	ACTIVE
1	2	3	4	5

AM
___
PM

SUNDAY

HIDING	**FISH BEHAVIOUR**	ACTIVE
1	2	3	4	5

AM
___
PM

TEST/ CHANGE / CHECK

/ /	AM PM	°C	DAYS SINCE LAST TEST

TEST

RESULT	:)	:(

NH₃ AMMONIA	ppm	:) ☐	:(☐
NO₂ NITRITE	ppm	:) ☐	:(☐
NO₃ NITRATE	ppm	:) ☐	:(☐
pH	pH	:) ☐	:(☐

CHECK

FILTERS

CHECKED ☐	CLEANED ☐	**OR**	CHANGED ☐

PUMP	CHECKED ☐
AIRLINE	CHECKED ☐
LIGHTING	CHECKED ☐

CHANGE

NOTE WATER CHANGED AFTER TEST AS A PERCENTAGE

%

WATER TEST/ CHANGE NOTES

FISH COUNT

#

| **WEEK BEGINNING:** / / | **FEED TIMES** |

MONDAY *ADD DAILY NOTES AND OBSERVATIONS*

| HIDING | **FISH BEHAVIOUR** | ACTIVE |
| 1 | 2 | 3 | 4 | 5 |

AM
___
PM

TUESDAY

| HIDING | **FISH BEHAVIOUR** | ACTIVE |
| 1 | 2 | 3 | 4 | 5 |

AM
___
PM

WEDNESDAY

| HIDING | **FISH BEHAVIOUR** | ACTIVE |
| 1 | 2 | 3 | 4 | 5 |

AM
___
PM

THURSDAY

| HIDING | **FISH BEHAVIOUR** | ACTIVE |
| 1 | 2 | 3 | 4 | 5 |

AM
___
PM

FRIDAY

| HIDING | **FISH BEHAVIOUR** | ACTIVE |
| 1 | 2 | 3 | 4 | 5 |

AM
___
PM

SATURDAY

| HIDING | **FISH BEHAVIOUR** | ACTIVE |
| 1 | 2 | 3 | 4 | 5 |

AM
___
PM

SUNDAY

| HIDING | **FISH BEHAVIOUR** | ACTIVE |
| 1 | 2 | 3 | 4 | 5 |

AM
___
PM

TEST/ CHANGE / CHECK

| / / | AM PM | °C | DAYS SINCE LAST TEST | |

TEST

RESULT ☺ ☹

NH₃ AMMONIA		ppm	☺ ☐ ☹ ☐
NO₂ NITRITE		ppm	☺ ☐ ☹ ☐
NO₃ NITRATE		ppm	☺ ☐ ☹ ☐
pH		pH	☺ ☐ ☹ ☐

CHECK

FILTERS

| CHECKED ☐ | CLEANED ☐ | **OR** | CHANGED ☐ |

PUMP	CHECKED ☐
AIRLINE	CHECKED ☐
LIGHTING	CHECKED ☐

CHANGE   NOTE WATER CHANGED AFTER TEST AS A PERCENTAGE   %

WATER TEST/ CHANGE NOTES

FISH COUNT

\#

WEEK BEGINNING: / /

MONDAY *ADD DAILY NOTES AND OBSERVATIONS*

HIDING	FISH BEHAVIOUR			ACTIVE
1	2	3	4	5

AM
___
PM

TUESDAY

HIDING	FISH BEHAVIOUR			ACTIVE
1	2	3	4	5

AM
___
PM

WEDNESDAY

HIDING	FISH BEHAVIOUR			ACTIVE
1	2	3	4	5

AM
___
PM

THURSDAY

HIDING	FISH BEHAVIOUR			ACTIVE
1	2	3	4	5

AM
___
PM

FRIDAY

HIDING	FISH BEHAVIOUR			ACTIVE
1	2	3	4	5

AM
___
PM

SATURDAY

HIDING	FISH BEHAVIOUR			ACTIVE
1	2	3	4	5

AM
___
PM

SUNDAY

HIDING	FISH BEHAVIOUR			ACTIVE
1	2	3	4	5

AM
___
PM

TEST/ CHANGE / CHECK

/ /	AM PM	°C	DAYS SINCE LAST TEST

TEST

RESULT ☺ ☹

NH₃ AMMONIA	ppm	☺ ☐ ☹ ☐
NO₂ NITRITE	ppm	☺ ☐ ☹ ☐
NO₃ NITRATE	ppm	☺ ☐ ☹ ☐
pH	pH	☺ ☐ ☹ ☐

CHECK

FILTERS

CHECKED ☐	CLEANED ☐	OR	CHANGED ☐

PUMP	CHECKED ☐
AIRLINE	CHECKED ☐
LIGHTING	CHECKED ☐

CHANGE   NOTE WATER CHANGED AFTER TEST AS A PERCENTAGE   %

WATER TEST/ CHANGE NOTES

FISH COUNT
#

WEEK BEGINNING: / /	FEED TIMES

MONDAY *ADD DAILY NOTES AND OBSERVATIONS*

HIDING	**FISH BEHAVIOUR**	ACTIVE
1	2	3	4	5

AM
___
PM

TUESDAY

HIDING	**FISH BEHAVIOUR**	ACTIVE
1	2	3	4	5

AM
___
PM

WEDNESDAY

HIDING	**FISH BEHAVIOUR**	ACTIVE
1	2	3	4	5

AM
___
PM

THURSDAY

HIDING	**FISH BEHAVIOUR**	ACTIVE
1	2	3	4	5

AM
___
PM

FRIDAY

HIDING	**FISH BEHAVIOUR**	ACTIVE
1	2	3	4	5

AM
___
PM

SATURDAY

HIDING	**FISH BEHAVIOUR**	ACTIVE
1	2	3	4	5

AM
___
PM

SUNDAY

HIDING	**FISH BEHAVIOUR**	ACTIVE
1	2	3	4	5

AM
___
PM

TEST/ CHANGE / CHECK

			DAYS SINCE LAST TEST
/ /	AM PM	°C	

TEST

RESULT ☺ ☹

			☺ ☹
NH₃ AMMONIA		ppm	☺ ☹ ☐ ☐
NO₂ NITRITE		ppm	☺ ☹ ☐ ☐
NO₃ NITRATE		ppm	☺ ☹ ☐ ☐
pH		pH	☺ ☹ ☐ ☐

CHECK

FILTERS

CHECKED ☐	CLEANED ☐	OR	CHANGED ☐

PUMP	CHECKED ☐
AIRLINE	CHECKED ☐
LIGHTING	CHECKED ☐

CHANGE

NOTE WATER CHANGED AFTER TEST AS A PERCENTAGE

%

WATER TEST/ CHANGE NOTES

FISH COUNT

#

WEEK BEGINNING: / /	FEED TIMES

MONDAY *ADD DAILY NOTES AND OBSERVATIONS*

HIDING **FISH BEHAVIOUR** ACTIVE
| 1 | 2 | 3 | 4 | 5 |

AM
___
PM

TUESDAY

HIDING **FISH BEHAVIOUR** ACTIVE
| 1 | 2 | 3 | 4 | 5 |

AM
___
PM

WEDNESDAY

HIDING **FISH BEHAVIOUR** ACTIVE
| 1 | 2 | 3 | 4 | 5 |

AM
___
PM

THURSDAY

HIDING **FISH BEHAVIOUR** ACTIVE
| 1 | 2 | 3 | 4 | 5 |

AM
___
PM

FRIDAY

HIDING **FISH BEHAVIOUR** ACTIVE
| 1 | 2 | 3 | 4 | 5 |

AM
___
PM

SATURDAY

HIDING **FISH BEHAVIOUR** ACTIVE
| 1 | 2 | 3 | 4 | 5 |

AM
___
PM

SUNDAY

HIDING **FISH BEHAVIOUR** ACTIVE
| 1 | 2 | 3 | 4 | 5 |

AM
___
PM

TEST/ CHANGE / CHECK

| / / | AM PM | °C | DAYS SINCE LAST TEST |

TEST

RESULT ☺ ☹

NH₃ AMMONIA		ppm	☺ ☐ ☹ ☐
NO₂ NITRITE		ppm	☺ ☐ ☹ ☐
NO₃ NITRATE		ppm	☺ ☐ ☹ ☐
pH		pH	☺ ☐ ☹ ☐

CHECK

FILTERS

| CHECKED ☐ | CLEANED ☐ | OR | CHANGED ☐ |

PUMP	CHECKED ☐
AIRLINE	CHECKED ☐
LIGHTING	CHECKED ☐

CHANGE   NOTE WATER CHANGED AFTER TEST AS A PERCENTAGE   %

WATER TEST/ CHANGE NOTES

FISH COUNT

#

WEEK BEGINNING: / /	FEED TIMES

MONDAY *ADD DAILY NOTES AND OBSERVATIONS*

HIDING	FISH BEHAVIOUR		ACTIVE
1	2	3	4	5

AM
___
PM

TUESDAY

HIDING	FISH BEHAVIOUR		ACTIVE
1	2	3	4	5

AM
___
PM

WEDNESDAY

HIDING	FISH BEHAVIOUR		ACTIVE
1	2	3	4	5

AM
___
PM

THURSDAY

HIDING	FISH BEHAVIOUR		ACTIVE
1	2	3	4	5

AM
___
PM

FRIDAY

HIDING	FISH BEHAVIOUR		ACTIVE
1	2	3	4	5

AM
___
PM

SATURDAY

HIDING	FISH BEHAVIOUR		ACTIVE
1	2	3	4	5

AM
___
PM

SUNDAY

HIDING	FISH BEHAVIOUR		ACTIVE
1	2	3	4	5

AM
___
PM

TEST/ CHANGE / CHECK

/ /	AM PM	°C	DAYS SINCE LAST TEST

TEST

RESULT ☺ ☹

		☺ ☹
NH₃ AMMONIA	ppm	☺ ☐ ☹ ☐
NO₂ NITRITE	ppm	☺ ☐ ☹ ☐
NO₃ NITRATE	ppm	☺ ☐ ☹ ☐
pH	pH	☺ ☐ ☹ ☐

CHECK

FILTERS

CHECKED ☐	CLEANED ☐	**OR**	CHANGED ☐

PUMP	CHECKED ☐
AIRLINE	CHECKED ☐
LIGHTING	CHECKED ☐

CHANGE   NOTE WATER CHANGED AFTER TEST AS A PERCENTAGE   %

WATER TEST/ CHANGE NOTES

FISH COUNT

#

WEEK BEGINNING: / /

MONDAY *ADD DAILY NOTES AND OBSERVATIONS*

HIDING **FISH BEHAVIOUR** ACTIVE
| 1 | 2 | 3 | 4 | 5 |

AM
___
PM

TUESDAY

HIDING **FISH BEHAVIOUR** ACTIVE
| 1 | 2 | 3 | 4 | 5 |

AM
___
PM

WEDNESDAY

HIDING **FISH BEHAVIOUR** ACTIVE
| 1 | 2 | 3 | 4 | 5 |

AM
___
PM

THURSDAY

HIDING **FISH BEHAVIOUR** ACTIVE
| 1 | 2 | 3 | 4 | 5 |

AM
___
PM

FRIDAY

HIDING **FISH BEHAVIOUR** ACTIVE
| 1 | 2 | 3 | 4 | 5 |

AM
___
PM

SATURDAY

HIDING **FISH BEHAVIOUR** ACTIVE
| 1 | 2 | 3 | 4 | 5 |

AM
___
PM

SUNDAY

HIDING **FISH BEHAVIOUR** ACTIVE
| 1 | 2 | 3 | 4 | 5 |

AM
___
PM

TEST/ CHANGE / CHECK

| / / | AM PM | °C | DAYS SINCE LAST TEST | |

TEST

| RESULT | ☺ | ☹ |

NH₃ AMMONIA		ppm	☺ ☐	☹ ☐
NO₂ NITRITE		ppm	☺ ☐	☹ ☐
NO₃ NITRATE		ppm	☺ ☐	☹ ☐
pH		pH	☺ ☐	☹ ☐

CHECK

FILTERS

| CHECKED ☐ | CLEANED ☐ | OR | CHANGED ☐ |

PUMP	CHECKED ☐
AIRLINE	CHECKED ☐
LIGHTING	CHECKED ☐

CHANGE

NOTE WATER CHANGED AFTER TEST AS A PERCENTAGE

%

WATER TEST/ CHANGE NOTES

FISH COUNT

#

WEEK BEGINNING: /   /

MONDAY *ADD DAILY NOTES AND OBSERVATIONS*

HIDING	FISH BEHAVIOUR			ACTIVE
1	2	3	4	5

AM
___
PM

TUESDAY

HIDING	FISH BEHAVIOUR			ACTIVE
1	2	3	4	5

AM
___
PM

WEDNESDAY

HIDING	FISH BEHAVIOUR			ACTIVE
1	2	3	4	5

AM
___
PM

THURSDAY

HIDING	FISH BEHAVIOUR			ACTIVE
1	2	3	4	5

AM
___
PM

FRIDAY

HIDING	FISH BEHAVIOUR			ACTIVE
1	2	3	4	5

AM
___
PM

SATURDAY

HIDING	FISH BEHAVIOUR			ACTIVE
1	2	3	4	5

AM
___
PM

SUNDAY

HIDING	FISH BEHAVIOUR			ACTIVE
1	2	3	4	5

AM
___
PM

TEST/ CHANGE / CHECK

| / / | AM PM | °C | DAYS SINCE LAST TEST |

TEST

RESULT	☺	☹

NH₃ AMMONIA	ppm	☺ ☐	☹ ☐
NO₂ NITRITE	ppm	☺ ☐	☹ ☐
NO₃ NITRATE	ppm	☺ ☐	☹ ☐
pH	pH	☺ ☐	☹ ☐

CHECK

FILTERS

| CHECKED ☐ | CLEANED ☐ | OR | CHANGED ☐ |

PUMP	CHECKED ☐
AIRLINE	CHECKED ☐
LIGHTING	CHECKED ☐

CHANGE

NOTE WATER CHANGED AFTER TEST AS A PERCENTAGE

%

WATER TEST/ CHANGE NOTES

FISH COUNT

#

WEEK BEGINNING: /   /

MONDAY *ADD DAILY NOTES AND OBSERVATIONS*

HIDING	**FISH BEHAVIOUR**			ACTIVE
1	2	3	4	5

AM
___
PM

TUESDAY

HIDING	**FISH BEHAVIOUR**			ACTIVE
1	2	3	4	5

AM
___
PM

WEDNESDAY

HIDING	**FISH BEHAVIOUR**			ACTIVE
1	2	3	4	5

AM
___
PM

THURSDAY

HIDING	**FISH BEHAVIOUR**			ACTIVE
1	2	3	4	5

AM
___
PM

FRIDAY

HIDING	**FISH BEHAVIOUR**			ACTIVE
1	2	3	4	5

AM
___
PM

SATURDAY

HIDING	**FISH BEHAVIOUR**			ACTIVE
1	2	3	4	5

AM
___
PM

SUNDAY

HIDING	**FISH BEHAVIOUR**			ACTIVE
1	2	3	4	5

AM
___
PM

TEST/ CHANGE / CHECK

/ /	AM PM	°C	DAYS SINCE LAST TEST

TEST

RESULT	☺	☹

NH₃ AMMONIA		ppm	☺ ☐	☹ ☐
NO₂ NITRITE		ppm	☺ ☐	☹ ☐
NO₃ NITRATE		ppm	☺ ☐	☹ ☐
pH		pH	☺ ☐	☹ ☐

CHECK

FILTERS

CHECKED ☐	CLEANED ☐	OR	CHANGED ☐

PUMP	CHECKED ☐
AIRLINE	CHECKED ☐
LIGHTING	CHECKED ☐

CHANGE

NOTE WATER CHANGED AFTER TEST AS A PERCENTAGE

%

WATER TEST/ CHANGE NOTES

FISH COUNT

#

WEEK BEGINNING: / /

MONDAY
ADD DAILY NOTES AND OBSERVATIONS

HIDING | **FISH BEHAVIOUR** | ACTIVE
1 | 2 | 3 | 4 | 5

AM
___
PM

TUESDAY

HIDING | **FISH BEHAVIOUR** | ACTIVE
1 | 2 | 3 | 4 | 5

AM
___
PM

WEDNESDAY

HIDING | **FISH BEHAVIOUR** | ACTIVE
1 | 2 | 3 | 4 | 5

AM
___
PM

THURSDAY

HIDING | **FISH BEHAVIOUR** | ACTIVE
1 | 2 | 3 | 4 | 5

AM
___
PM

FRIDAY

HIDING | **FISH BEHAVIOUR** | ACTIVE
1 | 2 | 3 | 4 | 5

AM
___
PM

SATURDAY

HIDING | **FISH BEHAVIOUR** | ACTIVE
1 | 2 | 3 | 4 | 5

AM
___
PM

SUNDAY

HIDING | **FISH BEHAVIOUR** | ACTIVE
1 | 2 | 3 | 4 | 5

AM
___
PM

TEST/ CHANGE / CHECK

/ /		AM PM	°C	DAYS SINCE LAST TEST

TEST

RESULT ☺ ☹

			☺ ☹
NH₃ AMMONIA		ppm	☺ ☐ ☹ ☐
NO₂ NITRITE		ppm	☺ ☐ ☹ ☐
NO₃ NITRATE		ppm	☺ ☐ ☹ ☐
pH		pH	☺ ☐ ☹ ☐

CHECK

FILTERS

CHECKED ☐	CLEANED ☐	OR	CHANGED ☐

PUMP	CHECKED ☐
AIRLINE	CHECKED ☐
LIGHTING	CHECKED ☐

CHANGE   NOTE WATER CHANGED AFTER TEST AS A PERCENTAGE   %

WATER TEST/ CHANGE NOTES

FISH COUNT

#

WEEK BEGINNING: / /	FEED TIMES

MONDAY *ADD DAILY NOTES AND OBSERVATIONS*

HIDING	**FISH BEHAVIOUR**	ACTIVE
1	2	3	4	5

AM
___
PM

TUESDAY

HIDING	**FISH BEHAVIOUR**	ACTIVE
1	2	3	4	5

AM
___
PM

WEDNESDAY

HIDING	**FISH BEHAVIOUR**	ACTIVE
1	2	3	4	5

AM
___
PM

THURSDAY

HIDING	**FISH BEHAVIOUR**	ACTIVE
1	2	3	4	5

AM
___
PM

FRIDAY

HIDING	**FISH BEHAVIOUR**	ACTIVE
1	2	3	4	5

AM
___
PM

SATURDAY

HIDING	**FISH BEHAVIOUR**	ACTIVE
1	2	3	4	5

AM
___
PM

SUNDAY

HIDING	**FISH BEHAVIOUR**	ACTIVE
1	2	3	4	5

AM
___
PM

TEST/ CHANGE / CHECK

/ /	AM PM	°C	DAYS SINCE LAST TEST

TEST

RESULT ☺ ☹

NH₃ AMMONIA	_____ ppm	☺ ☹ ☐ ☐
NO₂ NITRITE	_____ ppm	☺ ☹ ☐ ☐
NO₃ NITRATE	_____ ppm	☺ ☹ ☐ ☐
pH	_____ pH	☺ ☹ ☐ ☐

CHECK

FILTERS

CHECKED ☐	CLEANED ☐	OR	CHANGED ☐

PUMP	CHECKED ☐
AIRLINE	CHECKED ☐
LIGHTING	CHECKED ☐

CHANGE   NOTE WATER CHANGED AFTER TEST AS A PERCENTAGE   [%]

WATER TEST/ CHANGE NOTES

FISH COUNT
#

WEEK BEGINNING: / /	FEED TIMES

MONDAY *ADD DAILY NOTES AND OBSERVATIONS*

	HIDING	FISH BEHAVIOUR			ACTIVE	AM
	1	2	3	4	5	PM

TUESDAY

	HIDING	FISH BEHAVIOUR			ACTIVE	AM
	1	2	3	4	5	PM

WEDNESDAY

	HIDING	FISH BEHAVIOUR			ACTIVE	AM
	1	2	3	4	5	PM

THURSDAY

	HIDING	FISH BEHAVIOUR			ACTIVE	AM
	1	2	3	4	5	PM

FRIDAY

	HIDING	FISH BEHAVIOUR			ACTIVE	AM
	1	2	3	4	5	PM

SATURDAY

	HIDING	FISH BEHAVIOUR			ACTIVE	AM
	1	2	3	4	5	PM

SUNDAY

	HIDING	FISH BEHAVIOUR			ACTIVE	AM
	1	2	3	4	5	PM

TEST/ CHANGE / CHECK

/ /	AM PM	°C	DAYS SINCE LAST TEST

TEST

RESULT ☺ ☹

NH₃ AMMONIA	ppm	☺ ☐ ☹ ☐
NO₂ NITRITE	ppm	☺ ☐ ☹ ☐
NO₃ NITRATE	ppm	☺ ☐ ☹ ☐
pH	pH	☺ ☐ ☹ ☐

CHECK

FILTERS

CHECKED ☐	CLEANED ☐	**OR**	CHANGED ☐

PUMP	CHECKED ☐
AIRLINE	CHECKED ☐
LIGHTING	CHECKED ☐

CHANGE   NOTE WATER CHANGED AFTER TEST AS A PERCENTAGE   [%]

WATER TEST/ CHANGE NOTES

FISH COUNT

#

WEEK BEGINNING: / /	**FEED TIMES**

MONDAY *ADD DAILY NOTES AND OBSERVATIONS*

HIDING	**FISH BEHAVIOUR**	ACTIVE
1	2	3	4	5

AM
___
PM

TUESDAY

HIDING	**FISH BEHAVIOUR**	ACTIVE
1	2	3	4	5

AM
___
PM

WEDNESDAY

HIDING	**FISH BEHAVIOUR**	ACTIVE
1	2	3	4	5

AM
___
PM

THURSDAY

HIDING	**FISH BEHAVIOUR**	ACTIVE
1	2	3	4	5

AM
___
PM

FRIDAY

HIDING	**FISH BEHAVIOUR**	ACTIVE
1	2	3	4	5

AM
___
PM

SATURDAY

HIDING	**FISH BEHAVIOUR**	ACTIVE
1	2	3	4	5

AM
___
PM

SUNDAY

HIDING	**FISH BEHAVIOUR**	ACTIVE
1	2	3	4	5

AM
___
PM

TEST/ CHANGE / CHECK

/ /	AM PM	°C	DAYS SINCE LAST TEST

TEST

RESULT	☺ ☹

NH$_3$ AMMONIA	ppm	☺ ☐ ☹ ☐
NO$_2$ NITRITE	ppm	☺ ☐ ☹ ☐
NO$_3$ NITRATE	ppm	☺ ☐ ☹ ☐
pH	pH	☺ ☐ ☹ ☐

CHECK

FILTERS

CHECKED ☐	CLEANED ☐	OR	CHANGED ☐

PUMP	CHECKED ☐
AIRLINE	CHECKED ☐
LIGHTING	CHECKED ☐

CHANGE

NOTE WATER CHANGED AFTER TEST AS A PERCENTAGE

%

WATER TEST/ CHANGE NOTES

FISH COUNT

#

WEEK BEGINNING: / /

MONDAY
ADD DAILY NOTES AND OBSERVATIONS

HIDING	**FISH BEHAVIOUR**			ACTIVE
1	2	3	4	5

AM
___
PM

TUESDAY

HIDING	**FISH BEHAVIOUR**			ACTIVE
1	2	3	4	5

AM
___
PM

WEDNESDAY

HIDING	**FISH BEHAVIOUR**			ACTIVE
1	2	3	4	5

AM
___
PM

THURSDAY

HIDING	**FISH BEHAVIOUR**			ACTIVE
1	2	3	4	5

AM
___
PM

FRIDAY

HIDING	**FISH BEHAVIOUR**			ACTIVE
1	2	3	4	5

AM
___
PM

SATURDAY

HIDING	**FISH BEHAVIOUR**			ACTIVE
1	2	3	4	5

AM
___
PM

SUNDAY

HIDING	**FISH BEHAVIOUR**			ACTIVE
1	2	3	4	5

AM
___
PM

TEST/ CHANGE / CHECK

| /   / | AM PM | °C | DAYS SINCE LAST TEST |

TEST

RESULT ☺ ☹

NH₃ AMMONIA		ppm	☺ ☐ ☹ ☐
NO₂ NITRITE		ppm	☺ ☐ ☹ ☐
NO₃ NITRATE		ppm	☺ ☐ ☹ ☐
pH		pH	☺ ☐ ☹ ☐

CHECK

FILTERS

| CHECKED ☐ | CLEANED ☐ | **OR** | CHANGED ☐ |

PUMP	CHECKED ☐
AIRLINE	CHECKED ☐
LIGHTING	CHECKED ☐

CHANGE   NOTE WATER CHANGED AFTER TEST AS A PERCENTAGE   %

WATER TEST/ CHANGE NOTES

FISH COUNT

#

WEEK BEGINNING: /   /

MONDAY *ADD DAILY NOTES AND OBSERVATIONS*

HIDING	FISH BEHAVIOUR			ACTIVE
1	2	3	4	5

AM
___
PM

TUESDAY

HIDING	FISH BEHAVIOUR			ACTIVE
1	2	3	4	5

AM
___
PM

WEDNESDAY

HIDING	FISH BEHAVIOUR			ACTIVE
1	2	3	4	5

AM
___
PM

THURSDAY

HIDING	FISH BEHAVIOUR			ACTIVE
1	2	3	4	5

AM
___
PM

FRIDAY

HIDING	FISH BEHAVIOUR			ACTIVE
1	2	3	4	5

AM
___
PM

SATURDAY

HIDING	FISH BEHAVIOUR			ACTIVE
1	2	3	4	5

AM
___
PM

SUNDAY

HIDING	FISH BEHAVIOUR			ACTIVE
1	2	3	4	5

AM
___
PM

TEST/ CHANGE / CHECK

/ /	AM PM	°C	DAYS SINCE LAST TEST

TEST

RESULT ☺ ☹

		☺ ☹
NH₃ AMMONIA	ppm	☺ ☐ ☹ ☐
NO₂ NITRITE	ppm	☺ ☐ ☹ ☐
NO₃ NITRATE	ppm	☺ ☐ ☹ ☐
pH	pH	☺ ☐ ☹ ☐

CHECK

FILTERS

CHECKED ☐	CLEANED ☐	OR	CHANGED ☐

PUMP	CHECKED ☐
AIRLINE	CHECKED ☐
LIGHTING	CHECKED ☐

CHANGE   NOTE WATER CHANGED AFTER TEST AS A PERCENTAGE   %

WATER TEST/ CHANGE NOTES

FISH COUNT

#

WEEK BEGINNING: / /	FEED TIMES

MONDAY   *ADD DAILY NOTES AND OBSERVATIONS*

HIDING **FISH BEHAVIOUR** ACTIVE
| 1 | 2 | 3 | 4 | 5 |

AM
—
PM

TUESDAY

HIDING **FISH BEHAVIOUR** ACTIVE
| 1 | 2 | 3 | 4 | 5 |

AM
—
PM

WEDNESDAY

HIDING **FISH BEHAVIOUR** ACTIVE
| 1 | 2 | 3 | 4 | 5 |

AM
—
PM

THURSDAY

HIDING **FISH BEHAVIOUR** ACTIVE
| 1 | 2 | 3 | 4 | 5 |

AM
—
PM

FRIDAY

HIDING **FISH BEHAVIOUR** ACTIVE
| 1 | 2 | 3 | 4 | 5 |

AM
—
PM

SATURDAY

HIDING **FISH BEHAVIOUR** ACTIVE
| 1 | 2 | 3 | 4 | 5 |

AM
—
PM

SUNDAY

HIDING **FISH BEHAVIOUR** ACTIVE
| 1 | 2 | 3 | 4 | 5 |

AM
—
PM

TEST/ CHANGE / CHECK

| / / | AM
PM | °C | DAYS
SINCE
LAST TEST |

TEST

RESULT ☺ ☹

NH₃ AMMONIA	ppm	☺ ☹
NO₂ NITRITE	ppm	☺ ☹
NO₃ NITRATE	ppm	☺ ☹
pH	pH	☺ ☹

CHECK

FILTERS

| CHECKED ☐ | CLEANED ☐ | **OR** | CHANGED ☐ |

PUMP	CHECKED ☐
AIRLINE	CHECKED ☐
LIGHTING	CHECKED ☐

CHANGE   NOTE WATER CHANGED AFTER TEST AS A PERCENTAGE   %

WATER TEST/ CHANGE NOTES

FISH COUNT
#

WEEK BEGINNING: / /	FEED TIMES

MONDAY *ADD DAILY NOTES AND OBSERVATIONS*

HIDING **FISH BEHAVIOUR** ACTIVE
| 1 | 2 | 3 | 4 | 5 |

AM
___
PM

TUESDAY

HIDING **FISH BEHAVIOUR** ACTIVE
| 1 | 2 | 3 | 4 | 5 |

AM
___
PM

WEDNESDAY

HIDING **FISH BEHAVIOUR** ACTIVE
| 1 | 2 | 3 | 4 | 5 |

AM
___
PM

THURSDAY

HIDING **FISH BEHAVIOUR** ACTIVE
| 1 | 2 | 3 | 4 | 5 |

AM
___
PM

FRIDAY

HIDING **FISH BEHAVIOUR** ACTIVE
| 1 | 2 | 3 | 4 | 5 |

AM
___
PM

SATURDAY

HIDING **FISH BEHAVIOUR** ACTIVE
| 1 | 2 | 3 | 4 | 5 |

AM
___
PM

SUNDAY

HIDING **FISH BEHAVIOUR** ACTIVE
| 1 | 2 | 3 | 4 | 5 |

AM
___
PM

TEST/ CHANGE / CHECK

/ /	AM PM	°C	DAYS SINCE LAST TEST

TEST

RESULT	☺	☹

NH₃ AMMONIA		ppm	☺ ☐	☹ ☐
NO₂ NITRITE		ppm	☺ ☐	☹ ☐
NO₃ NITRATE		ppm	☺ ☐	☹ ☐
pH		pH	☺ ☐	☹ ☐

CHECK

FILTERS

CHECKED ☐	CLEANED ☐	**OR**	CHANGED ☐

PUMP	CHECKED ☐
AIRLINE	CHECKED ☐
LIGHTING	CHECKED ☐

CHANGE

NOTE WATER CHANGED AFTER TEST AS A PERCENTAGE

%

WATER TEST/ CHANGE NOTES

FISH COUNT

#

WEEK BEGINNING: / /	FEED TIMES

MONDAY *ADD DAILY NOTES AND OBSERVATIONS*

HIDING	FISH BEHAVIOUR			ACTIVE
1	2	3	4	5

AM
___
PM

TUESDAY

HIDING	FISH BEHAVIOUR			ACTIVE
1	2	3	4	5

AM
___
PM

WEDNESDAY

HIDING	FISH BEHAVIOUR			ACTIVE
1	2	3	4	5

AM
___
PM

THURSDAY

HIDING	FISH BEHAVIOUR			ACTIVE
1	2	3	4	5

AM
___
PM

FRIDAY

HIDING	FISH BEHAVIOUR			ACTIVE
1	2	3	4	5

AM
___
PM

SATURDAY

HIDING	FISH BEHAVIOUR			ACTIVE
1	2	3	4	5

AM
___
PM

SUNDAY

HIDING	FISH BEHAVIOUR			ACTIVE
1	2	3	4	5

AM
___
PM

TEST/ CHANGE / CHECK

	/	/		AM PM		°C	DAYS SINCE LAST TEST	

TEST

RESULT ☺ ☹

NH$_3$ AMMONIA	ppm	☺ ☹ ☐ ☐
NO$_2$ NITRITE	ppm	☺ ☹ ☐ ☐
NO$_3$ NITRATE	ppm	☺ ☹ ☐ ☐
pH	pH	☺ ☹ ☐ ☐

CHECK

FILTERS

CHECKED ☐	CLEANED ☐	**OR**	CHANGED ☐

PUMP	CHECKED ☐
AIRLINE	CHECKED ☐
LIGHTING	CHECKED ☐

CHANGE   NOTE WATER CHANGED AFTER TEST AS A PERCENTAGE   %

WATER TEST/ CHANGE NOTES

FISH COUNT

#

WEEK BEGINNING: / /	FEED TIMES

MONDAY *ADD DAILY NOTES AND OBSERVATIONS*

HIDING	**FISH BEHAVIOUR**			ACTIVE
1	2	3	4	5

AM
___
PM

TUESDAY

HIDING	**FISH BEHAVIOUR**			ACTIVE
1	2	3	4	5

AM
___
PM

WEDNESDAY

HIDING	**FISH BEHAVIOUR**			ACTIVE
1	2	3	4	5

AM
___
PM

THURSDAY

HIDING	**FISH BEHAVIOUR**			ACTIVE
1	2	3	4	5

AM
___
PM

FRIDAY

HIDING	**FISH BEHAVIOUR**			ACTIVE
1	2	3	4	5

AM
___
PM

SATURDAY

HIDING	**FISH BEHAVIOUR**			ACTIVE
1	2	3	4	5

AM
___
PM

SUNDAY

HIDING	**FISH BEHAVIOUR**			ACTIVE
1	2	3	4	5

AM
___
PM

TEST/ CHANGE / CHECK

/ /	AM PM	°C	DAYS SINCE LAST TEST

TEST

RESULT ☺ ☹

NH₃ AMMONIA	____ ppm	☺ ☐ ☹ ☐
NO₂ NITRITE	____ ppm	☺ ☐ ☹ ☐
NO₃ NITRATE	____ ppm	☺ ☐ ☹ ☐
pH	____ pH	☺ ☐ ☹ ☐

CHECK

FILTERS

CHECKED ☐	CLEANED ☐	OR	CHANGED ☐

PUMP	CHECKED ☐
AIRLINE	CHECKED ☐
LIGHTING	CHECKED ☐

CHANGE
NOTE WATER CHANGED AFTER TEST AS A PERCENTAGE
%

WATER TEST/ CHANGE NOTES

FISH COUNT
#

WEEK BEGINNING: / /	**FEED TIMES**

MONDAY *ADD DAILY NOTES AND OBSERVATIONS*

HIDING **FISH BEHAVIOUR** ACTIVE
| 1 | 2 | 3 | 4 | 5 |

AM
___
PM

TUESDAY

HIDING **FISH BEHAVIOUR** ACTIVE
| 1 | 2 | 3 | 4 | 5 |

AM
___
PM

WEDNESDAY

HIDING **FISH BEHAVIOUR** ACTIVE
| 1 | 2 | 3 | 4 | 5 |

AM
___
PM

THURSDAY

HIDING **FISH BEHAVIOUR** ACTIVE
| 1 | 2 | 3 | 4 | 5 |

AM
___
PM

FRIDAY

HIDING **FISH BEHAVIOUR** ACTIVE
| 1 | 2 | 3 | 4 | 5 |

AM
___
PM

SATURDAY

HIDING **FISH BEHAVIOUR** ACTIVE
| 1 | 2 | 3 | 4 | 5 |

AM
___
PM

SUNDAY

HIDING **FISH BEHAVIOUR** ACTIVE
| 1 | 2 | 3 | 4 | 5 |

AM
___
PM

TEST/ CHANGE / CHECK

/ /	AM PM	°C	DAYS SINCE LAST TEST

TEST

RESULT ☺ ☹

		☺ ☹
NH₃ AMMONIA	_____ ppm	☺ ☐ ☹ ☐
NO₂ NITRITE	_____ ppm	☺ ☐ ☹ ☐
NO₃ NITRATE	_____ ppm	☺ ☐ ☹ ☐
pH	_____ pH	☺ ☐ ☹ ☐

CHECK

FILTERS

CHECKED ☐	CLEANED ☐	OR	CHANGED ☐

PUMP	CHECKED ☐
AIRLINE	CHECKED ☐
LIGHTING	CHECKED ☐

CHANGE

NOTE WATER CHANGED AFTER TEST AS A PERCENTAGE

%

WATER TEST/ CHANGE NOTES

FISH COUNT

#

WEEK BEGINNING: /   /

MONDAY   *ADD DAILY NOTES AND OBSERVATIONS*

HIDING	**FISH BEHAVIOUR**			ACTIVE
1	2	3	4	5

AM
___
PM

TUESDAY

HIDING	**FISH BEHAVIOUR**			ACTIVE
1	2	3	4	5

AM
___
PM

WEDNESDAY

HIDING	**FISH BEHAVIOUR**			ACTIVE
1	2	3	4	5

AM
___
PM

THURSDAY

HIDING	**FISH BEHAVIOUR**			ACTIVE
1	2	3	4	5

AM
___
PM

FRIDAY

HIDING	**FISH BEHAVIOUR**			ACTIVE
1	2	3	4	5

AM
___
PM

SATURDAY

HIDING	**FISH BEHAVIOUR**			ACTIVE
1	2	3	4	5

AM
___
PM

SUNDAY

HIDING	**FISH BEHAVIOUR**			ACTIVE
1	2	3	4	5

AM
___
PM

TEST/ CHANGE / CHECK

/ /	AM PM	°C	DAYS SINCE LAST TEST

TEST

RESULT	☺	☹

NH₃ AMMONIA		ppm	☺ ☐	☹ ☐
NO₂ NITRITE		ppm	☺ ☐	☹ ☐
NO₃ NITRATE		ppm	☺ ☐	☹ ☐
pH		pH	☺ ☐	☹ ☐

CHECK

FILTERS

CHECKED ☐	CLEANED ☐	OR	CHANGED ☐

PUMP	CHECKED ☐
AIRLINE	CHECKED ☐
LIGHTING	CHECKED ☐

CHANGE

NOTE WATER CHANGED AFTER TEST AS A PERCENTAGE

%

WATER TEST/ CHANGE NOTES

FISH COUNT

#

WEEK BEGINNING: / /	FEED TIMES

MONDAY *ADD DAILY NOTES AND OBSERVATIONS*

HIDING **FISH BEHAVIOUR** ACTIVE
| 1 | 2 | 3 | 4 | 5 |

AM
___
PM

TUESDAY

HIDING **FISH BEHAVIOUR** ACTIVE
| 1 | 2 | 3 | 4 | 5 |

AM
___
PM

WEDNESDAY

HIDING **FISH BEHAVIOUR** ACTIVE
| 1 | 2 | 3 | 4 | 5 |

AM
___
PM

THURSDAY

HIDING **FISH BEHAVIOUR** ACTIVE
| 1 | 2 | 3 | 4 | 5 |

AM
___
PM

FRIDAY

HIDING **FISH BEHAVIOUR** ACTIVE
| 1 | 2 | 3 | 4 | 5 |

AM
___
PM

SATURDAY

HIDING **FISH BEHAVIOUR** ACTIVE
| 1 | 2 | 3 | 4 | 5 |

AM
___
PM

SUNDAY

HIDING **FISH BEHAVIOUR** ACTIVE
| 1 | 2 | 3 | 4 | 5 |

AM
___
PM

TEST/ CHANGE / CHECK

/ /	AM PM	°C	DAYS SINCE LAST TEST

TEST

RESULT ☺ ☹

NH₃ AMMONIA	ppm	☺ ☐	☹ ☐
NO₂ NITRITE	ppm	☺ ☐	☹ ☐
NO₃ NITRATE	ppm	☺ ☐	☹ ☐
pH	pH	☺ ☐	☹ ☐

CHECK

FILTERS

CHECKED ☐	CLEANED ☐	OR	CHANGED ☐

PUMP	CHECKED ☐
AIRLINE	CHECKED ☐
LIGHTING	CHECKED ☐

CHANGE

NOTE WATER CHANGED AFTER TEST AS A PERCENTAGE

%

WATER TEST/ CHANGE NOTES

FISH COUNT

#

WEEK BEGINNING: / /	**FEED TIMES**

MONDAY *ADD DAILY NOTES AND OBSERVATIONS*

HIDING	**FISH BEHAVIOUR**	ACTIVE
1	2	3	4	5

AM
___
PM

TUESDAY

HIDING	**FISH BEHAVIOUR**	ACTIVE
1	2	3	4	5

AM
___
PM

WEDNESDAY

HIDING	**FISH BEHAVIOUR**	ACTIVE
1	2	3	4	5

AM
___
PM

THURSDAY

HIDING	**FISH BEHAVIOUR**	ACTIVE
1	2	3	4	5

AM
___
PM

FRIDAY

HIDING	**FISH BEHAVIOUR**	ACTIVE
1	2	3	4	5

AM
___
PM

SATURDAY

HIDING	**FISH BEHAVIOUR**	ACTIVE
1	2	3	4	5

AM
___
PM

SUNDAY

HIDING	**FISH BEHAVIOUR**	ACTIVE
1	2	3	4	5

AM
___
PM

TEST/ CHANGE / CHECK

/ /	AM PM	°C	DAYS SINCE LAST TEST

TEST

RESULT ☺ ☹

NH₃ AMMONIA	ppm	☺ ☹ ☐ ☐
NO₂ NITRITE	ppm	☺ ☹ ☐ ☐
NO₃ NITRATE	ppm	☺ ☹ ☐ ☐
pH	pH	☺ ☹ ☐ ☐

CHECK

FILTERS

CHECKED ☐	CLEANED ☐	OR	CHANGED ☐

PUMP	CHECKED ☐
AIRLINE	CHECKED ☐
LIGHTING	CHECKED ☐

CHANGE

NOTE WATER CHANGED AFTER TEST AS A PERCENTAGE

%

WATER TEST/ CHANGE NOTES

FISH COUNT

#

WEEK BEGINNING: / /	FEED TIMES

MONDAY *ADD DAILY NOTES AND OBSERVATIONS*

HIDING **FISH BEHAVIOUR** ACTIVE
| 1 | 2 | 3 | 4 | 5 |

AM
___
PM

TUESDAY

HIDING **FISH BEHAVIOUR** ACTIVE
| 1 | 2 | 3 | 4 | 5 |

AM
___
PM

WEDNESDAY

HIDING **FISH BEHAVIOUR** ACTIVE
| 1 | 2 | 3 | 4 | 5 |

AM
___
PM

THURSDAY

HIDING **FISH BEHAVIOUR** ACTIVE
| 1 | 2 | 3 | 4 | 5 |

AM
___
PM

FRIDAY

HIDING **FISH BEHAVIOUR** ACTIVE
| 1 | 2 | 3 | 4 | 5 |

AM
___
PM

SATURDAY

HIDING **FISH BEHAVIOUR** ACTIVE
| 1 | 2 | 3 | 4 | 5 |

AM
___
PM

SUNDAY

HIDING **FISH BEHAVIOUR** ACTIVE
| 1 | 2 | 3 | 4 | 5 |

AM
___
PM

TEST/ CHANGE / CHECK

/ /	AM PM	°C	DAYS SINCE LAST TEST

TEST

RESULT ☺ ☹

NH₃ AMMONIA	ppm	☺ ☐ ☹ ☐
NO₂ NITRITE	ppm	☺ ☐ ☹ ☐
NO₃ NITRATE	ppm	☺ ☐ ☹ ☐
pH	pH	☺ ☐ ☹ ☐

CHECK

FILTERS

CHECKED ☐	CLEANED ☐	OR	CHANGED ☐

PUMP	CHECKED ☐
AIRLINE	CHECKED ☐
LIGHTING	CHECKED ☐

CHANGE   NOTE WATER CHANGED AFTER TEST AS A PERCENTAGE   %

WATER TEST/ CHANGE NOTES

FISH COUNT
#

WEEK BEGINNING: /   /

MONDAY *ADD DAILY NOTES AND OBSERVATIONS*

HIDING **FISH BEHAVIOUR** ACTIVE
| 1 | 2 | 3 | 4 | 5 |

AM
___
PM

TUESDAY

HIDING **FISH BEHAVIOUR** ACTIVE
| 1 | 2 | 3 | 4 | 5 |

AM
___
PM

WEDNESDAY

HIDING **FISH BEHAVIOUR** ACTIVE
| 1 | 2 | 3 | 4 | 5 |

AM
___
PM

THURSDAY

HIDING **FISH BEHAVIOUR** ACTIVE
| 1 | 2 | 3 | 4 | 5 |

AM
___
PM

FRIDAY

HIDING **FISH BEHAVIOUR** ACTIVE
| 1 | 2 | 3 | 4 | 5 |

AM
___
PM

SATURDAY

HIDING **FISH BEHAVIOUR** ACTIVE
| 1 | 2 | 3 | 4 | 5 |

AM
___
PM

SUNDAY

HIDING **FISH BEHAVIOUR** ACTIVE
| 1 | 2 | 3 | 4 | 5 |

AM
___
PM

TEST/ CHANGE / CHECK

| / / | | AM
PM | °C | DAYS
SINCE
LAST TEST | |

TEST

RESULT ☺ ☹

NH₃ AMMONIA		ppm	☺ ☐ ☹ ☐
NO₂ NITRITE		ppm	☺ ☐ ☹ ☐
NO₃ NITRATE		ppm	☺ ☐ ☹ ☐
pH		pH	☺ ☐ ☹ ☐

CHECK

FILTERS

| CHECKED
☐ | CLEANED
☐ | **OR** | CHANGED
☐ |

PUMP	CHECKED ☐
AIRLINE	CHECKED ☐
LIGHTING	CHECKED ☐

CHANGE

NOTE WATER CHANGED AFTER TEST AS A PERCENTAGE

%

WATER TEST/ CHANGE NOTES

FISH COUNT

#

WEEK BEGINNING: / /	**FEED TIMES**

MONDAY *ADD DAILY NOTES AND OBSERVATIONS*

HIDING **FISH BEHAVIOUR** ACTIVE
| 1 | 2 | 3 | 4 | 5 |

AM
___
PM

TUESDAY

HIDING **FISH BEHAVIOUR** ACTIVE
| 1 | 2 | 3 | 4 | 5 |

AM
___
PM

WEDNESDAY

HIDING **FISH BEHAVIOUR** ACTIVE
| 1 | 2 | 3 | 4 | 5 |

AM
___
PM

THURSDAY

HIDING **FISH BEHAVIOUR** ACTIVE
| 1 | 2 | 3 | 4 | 5 |

AM
___
PM

FRIDAY

HIDING **FISH BEHAVIOUR** ACTIVE
| 1 | 2 | 3 | 4 | 5 |

AM
___
PM

SATURDAY

HIDING **FISH BEHAVIOUR** ACTIVE
| 1 | 2 | 3 | 4 | 5 |

AM
___
PM

SUNDAY

HIDING **FISH BEHAVIOUR** ACTIVE
| 1 | 2 | 3 | 4 | 5 |

AM
___
PM

TEST/ CHANGE / CHECK

/ /	AM PM	°C	DAYS SINCE LAST TEST

TEST

RESULT ☺ ☹

NH₃ AMMONIA	ppm	☺ ☐ ☹ ☐
NO₂ NITRITE	ppm	☺ ☐ ☹ ☐
NO₃ NITRATE	ppm	☺ ☐ ☹ ☐
pH pH		☺ ☐ ☹ ☐

CHECK

FILTERS

CHECKED ☐	CLEANED ☐	OR	CHANGED ☐

PUMP	CHECKED ☐
AIRLINE	CHECKED ☐
LIGHTING	CHECKED ☐

CHANGE   NOTE WATER CHANGED AFTER TEST AS A PERCENTAGE   %

WATER TEST/ CHANGE NOTES

FISH COUNT

#

WEEK BEGINNING: / /

MONDAY *ADD DAILY NOTES AND OBSERVATIONS*

HIDING **FISH BEHAVIOUR** ACTIVE
| 1 | 2 | 3 | 4 | 5 |

AM

PM

TUESDAY

HIDING **FISH BEHAVIOUR** ACTIVE
| 1 | 2 | 3 | 4 | 5 |

AM

PM

WEDNESDAY

HIDING **FISH BEHAVIOUR** ACTIVE
| 1 | 2 | 3 | 4 | 5 |

AM

PM

THURSDAY

HIDING **FISH BEHAVIOUR** ACTIVE
| 1 | 2 | 3 | 4 | 5 |

AM

PM

FRIDAY

HIDING **FISH BEHAVIOUR** ACTIVE
| 1 | 2 | 3 | 4 | 5 |

AM

PM

SATURDAY

HIDING **FISH BEHAVIOUR** ACTIVE
| 1 | 2 | 3 | 4 | 5 |

AM

PM

SUNDAY

HIDING **FISH BEHAVIOUR** ACTIVE
| 1 | 2 | 3 | 4 | 5 |

AM

PM

TEST/ CHANGE / CHECK

| / | / | | AM PM | | °C | DAYS SINCE LAST TEST | |

TEST

RESULT ☺ ☹

NH$_3$ AMMONIA		ppm	☺ ☐	☹ ☐
NO$_2$ NITRITE		ppm	☺ ☐	☹ ☐
NO$_3$ NITRATE		ppm	☺ ☐	☹ ☐
pH		pH	☺ ☐	☹ ☐

CHECK

FILTERS

| CHECKED ☐ | CLEANED ☐ | OR | CHANGED ☐ |

PUMP	CHECKED ☐
AIRLINE	CHECKED ☐
LIGHTING	CHECKED ☐

CHANGE

NOTE WATER CHANGED AFTER TEST AS A PERCENTAGE

%

WATER TEST/ CHANGE NOTES

FISH COUNT

#

WEEK BEGINNING: / /	FEED TIMES

MONDAY *ADD DAILY NOTES AND OBSERVATIONS*

HIDING   **FISH BEHAVIOUR**   ACTIVE
| 1 | 2 | 3 | 4 | 5 |

AM
___
PM

TUESDAY

HIDING   **FISH BEHAVIOUR**   ACTIVE
| 1 | 2 | 3 | 4 | 5 |

AM
___
PM

WEDNESDAY

HIDING   **FISH BEHAVIOUR**   ACTIVE
| 1 | 2 | 3 | 4 | 5 |

AM
___
PM

THURSDAY

HIDING   **FISH BEHAVIOUR**   ACTIVE
| 1 | 2 | 3 | 4 | 5 |

AM
___
PM

FRIDAY

HIDING   **FISH BEHAVIOUR**   ACTIVE
| 1 | 2 | 3 | 4 | 5 |

AM
___
PM

SATURDAY

HIDING   **FISH BEHAVIOUR**   ACTIVE
| 1 | 2 | 3 | 4 | 5 |

AM
___
PM

SUNDAY

HIDING   **FISH BEHAVIOUR**   ACTIVE
| 1 | 2 | 3 | 4 | 5 |

AM
___
PM

TEST/ CHANGE / CHECK

| / / | | AM PM | °C | DAYS SINCE LAST TEST |

TEST

RESULT ☺ ☹

NH₃ AMMONIA		ppm	☺ ☐ ☹ ☐
NO₂ NITRITE		ppm	☺ ☐ ☹ ☐
NO₃ NITRATE		ppm	☺ ☐ ☹ ☐
pH		pH	☺ ☐ ☹ ☐

CHECK

FILTERS

| CHECKED ☐ | CLEANED ☐ | OR | CHANGED ☐ |

PUMP	CHECKED ☐
AIRLINE	CHECKED ☐
LIGHTING	CHECKED ☐

CHANGE

NOTE WATER CHANGED AFTER TEST AS A PERCENTAGE

%

WATER TEST/ CHANGE NOTES

FISH COUNT

#

WEEK BEGINNING: / /	FEED TIMES

MONDAY *ADD DAILY NOTES AND OBSERVATIONS*

HIDING **FISH BEHAVIOUR** ACTIVE
1 2 3 4 5

AM

PM

TUESDAY

HIDING **FISH BEHAVIOUR** ACTIVE
1 2 3 4 5

AM

PM

WEDNESDAY

HIDING **FISH BEHAVIOUR** ACTIVE
1 2 3 4 5

AM

PM

THURSDAY

HIDING **FISH BEHAVIOUR** ACTIVE
1 2 3 4 5

AM

PM

FRIDAY

HIDING **FISH BEHAVIOUR** ACTIVE
1 2 3 4 5

AM

PM

SATURDAY

HIDING **FISH BEHAVIOUR** ACTIVE
1 2 3 4 5

AM

PM

SUNDAY

HIDING **FISH BEHAVIOUR** ACTIVE
1 2 3 4 5

AM

PM

TEST/ CHANGE / CHECK

| / / | AM PM | °C | DAYS SINCE LAST TEST |

TEST

RESULT ☺ ☹

NH₃ AMMONIA	ppm	☺ ☐ ☹ ☐
NO₂ NITRITE	ppm	☺ ☐ ☹ ☐
NO₃ NITRATE	ppm	☺ ☐ ☹ ☐
pH	pH	☺ ☐ ☹ ☐

CHECK

FILTERS

| CHECKED ☐ | CLEANED ☐ | OR | CHANGED ☐ |

PUMP	CHECKED ☐
AIRLINE	CHECKED ☐
LIGHTING	CHECKED ☐

CHANGE

NOTE WATER CHANGED AFTER TEST AS A PERCENTAGE

%

WATER TEST/ CHANGE NOTES

FISH COUNT

#

WEEK BEGINNING: / /	FEED TIMES

MONDAY *ADD DAILY NOTES AND OBSERVATIONS*

HIDING	**FISH BEHAVIOUR**	ACTIVE
1	2	3	4	5

AM
___
PM

TUESDAY

HIDING	**FISH BEHAVIOUR**	ACTIVE
1	2	3	4	5

AM
___
PM

WEDNESDAY

HIDING	**FISH BEHAVIOUR**	ACTIVE
1	2	3	4	5

AM
___
PM

THURSDAY

HIDING	**FISH BEHAVIOUR**	ACTIVE
1	2	3	4	5

AM
___
PM

FRIDAY

HIDING	**FISH BEHAVIOUR**	ACTIVE
1	2	3	4	5

AM
___
PM

SATURDAY

HIDING	**FISH BEHAVIOUR**	ACTIVE
1	2	3	4	5

AM
___
PM

SUNDAY

HIDING	**FISH BEHAVIOUR**	ACTIVE
1	2	3	4	5

AM
___
PM

TEST/ CHANGE / CHECK

/ /	AM PM	°C	DAYS SINCE LAST TEST

TEST

RESULT	☺	☹

NH₃ AMMONIA	ppm	☺ ☐	☹ ☐
NO₂ NITRITE	ppm	☺ ☐	☹ ☐
NO₃ NITRATE	ppm	☺ ☐	☹ ☐
pH	pH	☺ ☐	☹ ☐

CHECK

FILTERS

CHECKED ☐	CLEANED ☐	OR	CHANGED ☐

PUMP	CHECKED ☐
AIRLINE	CHECKED ☐
LIGHTING	CHECKED ☐

CHANGE NOTE WATER CHANGED AFTER TEST AS A PERCENTAGE   %

WATER TEST/ CHANGE NOTES

FISH COUNT
#

WEEK BEGINNING: /   /

MONDAY *ADD DAILY NOTES AND OBSERVATIONS*

HIDING	**FISH BEHAVIOUR**			ACTIVE
1	2	3	4	5

AM
___
PM

TUESDAY

HIDING	**FISH BEHAVIOUR**			ACTIVE
1	2	3	4	5

AM
___
PM

WEDNESDAY

HIDING	**FISH BEHAVIOUR**			ACTIVE
1	2	3	4	5

AM
___
PM

THURSDAY

HIDING	**FISH BEHAVIOUR**			ACTIVE
1	2	3	4	5

AM
___
PM

FRIDAY

HIDING	**FISH BEHAVIOUR**			ACTIVE
1	2	3	4	5

AM
___
PM

SATURDAY

HIDING	**FISH BEHAVIOUR**			ACTIVE
1	2	3	4	5

AM
___
PM

SUNDAY

HIDING	**FISH BEHAVIOUR**			ACTIVE
1	2	3	4	5

AM
___
PM

TEST/ CHANGE / CHECK

/ /	AM PM	°C	DAYS SINCE LAST TEST

TEST

RESULT ☺ ☹

NH₃ AMMONIA	ppm	☺ ☐ ☹ ☐
NO₂ NITRITE	ppm	☺ ☐ ☹ ☐
NO₃ NITRATE	ppm	☺ ☐ ☹ ☐
pH	pH	☺ ☐ ☹ ☐

CHECK

FILTERS

CHECKED ☐	CLEANED ☐	OR	CHANGED ☐

PUMP	CHECKED ☐
AIRLINE	CHECKED ☐
LIGHTING	CHECKED ☐

CHANGE

NOTE WATER CHANGED AFTER TEST AS A PERCENTAGE

%

WATER TEST/ CHANGE NOTES

FISH COUNT

#

WEEK BEGINNING: / /	FEED TIMES

MONDAY *ADD DAILY NOTES AND OBSERVATIONS*

	HIDING	**FISH BEHAVIOUR**			ACTIVE
	1	2	3	4	5

AM
___
PM

TUESDAY

	HIDING	**FISH BEHAVIOUR**			ACTIVE
	1	2	3	4	5

AM
___
PM

WEDNESDAY

	HIDING	**FISH BEHAVIOUR**			ACTIVE
	1	2	3	4	5

AM
___
PM

THURSDAY

	HIDING	**FISH BEHAVIOUR**			ACTIVE
	1	2	3	4	5

AM
___
PM

FRIDAY

	HIDING	**FISH BEHAVIOUR**			ACTIVE
	1	2	3	4	5

AM
___
PM

SATURDAY

	HIDING	**FISH BEHAVIOUR**			ACTIVE
	1	2	3	4	5

AM
___
PM

SUNDAY

	HIDING	**FISH BEHAVIOUR**			ACTIVE
	1	2	3	4	5

AM
___
PM

TEST/ CHANGE / CHECK

/ /		AM PM	°C	DAYS SINCE LAST TEST

TEST

RESULT ☺ ☹

NH₃ AMMONIA	_____ ppm	☺ ☐ ☹ ☐
NO₂ NITRITE	_____ ppm	☺ ☐ ☹ ☐
NO₃ NITRATE	_____ ppm	☺ ☐ ☹ ☐
pH	_____ pH	☺ ☐ ☹ ☐

CHECK

FILTERS

CHECKED ☐	CLEANED ☐	**OR**	CHANGED ☐

PUMP	CHECKED ☐
AIRLINE	CHECKED ☐
LIGHTING	CHECKED ☐

CHANGE   NOTE WATER CHANGED AFTER TEST AS A PERCENTAGE   %

WATER TEST/ CHANGE NOTES

FISH COUNT

#

WEEK BEGINNING: / /	FEED TIMES

MONDAY *ADD DAILY NOTES AND OBSERVATIONS*

HIDING **FISH BEHAVIOUR** ACTIVE
| 1 | 2 | 3 | 4 | 5 |

AM
___
PM

TUESDAY

HIDING **FISH BEHAVIOUR** ACTIVE
| 1 | 2 | 3 | 4 | 5 |

AM
___
PM

WEDNESDAY

HIDING **FISH BEHAVIOUR** ACTIVE
| 1 | 2 | 3 | 4 | 5 |

AM
___
PM

THURSDAY

HIDING **FISH BEHAVIOUR** ACTIVE
| 1 | 2 | 3 | 4 | 5 |

AM
___
PM

FRIDAY

HIDING **FISH BEHAVIOUR** ACTIVE
| 1 | 2 | 3 | 4 | 5 |

AM
___
PM

SATURDAY

HIDING **FISH BEHAVIOUR** ACTIVE
| 1 | 2 | 3 | 4 | 5 |

AM
___
PM

SUNDAY

HIDING **FISH BEHAVIOUR** ACTIVE
| 1 | 2 | 3 | 4 | 5 |

AM
___
PM

TEST/ CHANGE / CHECK

/ /	AM PM	°C	DAYS SINCE LAST TEST

TEST

RESULT ☺ ☹

NH₃ AMMONIA	ppm	☺ ☐ ☹ ☐
NO₂ NITRITE	ppm	☺ ☐ ☹ ☐
NO₃ NITRATE	ppm	☺ ☐ ☹ ☐
pH	pH	☺ ☐ ☹ ☐

CHECK

FILTERS

CHECKED ☐	CLEANED ☐	OR	CHANGED ☐

PUMP	CHECKED ☐
AIRLINE	CHECKED ☐
LIGHTING	CHECKED ☐

CHANGE

NOTE WATER CHANGED AFTER TEST AS A PERCENTAGE

%

WATER TEST/ CHANGE NOTES

FISH COUNT

#

WEEK BEGINNING: / /	FEED TIMES

MONDAY *ADD DAILY NOTES AND OBSERVATIONS*

HIDING	**FISH BEHAVIOUR**	ACTIVE
1	2	3	4	5

AM
___
PM

TUESDAY

HIDING	**FISH BEHAVIOUR**	ACTIVE
1	2	3	4	5

AM
___
PM

WEDNESDAY

HIDING	**FISH BEHAVIOUR**	ACTIVE
1	2	3	4	5

AM
___
PM

THURSDAY

HIDING	**FISH BEHAVIOUR**	ACTIVE
1	2	3	4	5

AM
___
PM

FRIDAY

HIDING	**FISH BEHAVIOUR**	ACTIVE
1	2	3	4	5

AM
___
PM

SATURDAY

HIDING	**FISH BEHAVIOUR**	ACTIVE
1	2	3	4	5

AM
___
PM

SUNDAY

HIDING	**FISH BEHAVIOUR**	ACTIVE
1	2	3	4	5

AM
___
PM

TEST/ CHANGE / CHECK

| / / | AM PM | °C | DAYS SINCE LAST TEST |

TEST

RESULT ☺ ☹

			☺ ☹
NH₃ AMMONIA		ppm	☺ ☹
NO₂ NITRITE		ppm	☺ ☹
NO₃ NITRATE		ppm	☺ ☹
pH		pH	☺ ☹

CHECK

FILTERS

| CHECKED ☐ | CLEANED ☐ | OR | CHANGED ☐ |

PUMP	CHECKED ☐
AIRLINE	CHECKED ☐
LIGHTING	CHECKED ☐

CHANGE

NOTE WATER CHANGED AFTER TEST AS A PERCENTAGE

%

WATER TEST/ CHANGE NOTES

FISH COUNT

#

WEEK BEGINNING: / /	**FEED TIMES**

MONDAY *ADD DAILY NOTES AND OBSERVATIONS*

HIDING **FISH BEHAVIOUR** ACTIVE
| 1 | 2 | 3 | 4 | 5 |

AM
___
PM

TUESDAY

HIDING **FISH BEHAVIOUR** ACTIVE
| 1 | 2 | 3 | 4 | 5 |

AM
___
PM

WEDNESDAY

HIDING **FISH BEHAVIOUR** ACTIVE
| 1 | 2 | 3 | 4 | 5 |

AM
___
PM

THURSDAY

HIDING **FISH BEHAVIOUR** ACTIVE
| 1 | 2 | 3 | 4 | 5 |

AM
___
PM

FRIDAY

HIDING **FISH BEHAVIOUR** ACTIVE
| 1 | 2 | 3 | 4 | 5 |

AM
___
PM

SATURDAY

HIDING **FISH BEHAVIOUR** ACTIVE
| 1 | 2 | 3 | 4 | 5 |

AM
___
PM

SUNDAY

HIDING **FISH BEHAVIOUR** ACTIVE
| 1 | 2 | 3 | 4 | 5 |

AM
___
PM

TEST/ CHANGE / CHECK

| / / | AM PM | °C | DAYS SINCE LAST TEST |

TEST

RESULT ☺ ☹

NH₃ AMMONIA		ppm	☺ ☐ ☹ ☐
NO₂ NITRITE		ppm	☺ ☐ ☹ ☐
NO₃ NITRATE		ppm	☺ ☐ ☹ ☐
pH		pH	☺ ☐ ☹ ☐

CHECK

FILTERS

| CHECKED ☐ | CLEANED ☐ | OR | CHANGED ☐ |

PUMP	CHECKED ☐
AIRLINE	CHECKED ☐
LIGHTING	CHECKED ☐

CHANGE   NOTE WATER CHANGED AFTER TEST AS A PERCENTAGE   %

WATER TEST/ CHANGE NOTES

FISH COUNT
#

WEEK BEGINNING: /   /

MONDAY   *ADD DAILY NOTES AND OBSERVATIONS*

HIDING **FISH BEHAVIOUR** ACTIVE
| 1 | 2 | 3 | 4 | 5 |

AM
___
PM

TUESDAY

HIDING **FISH BEHAVIOUR** ACTIVE
| 1 | 2 | 3 | 4 | 5 |

AM
___
PM

WEDNESDAY

HIDING **FISH BEHAVIOUR** ACTIVE
| 1 | 2 | 3 | 4 | 5 |

AM
___
PM

THURSDAY

HIDING **FISH BEHAVIOUR** ACTIVE
| 1 | 2 | 3 | 4 | 5 |

AM
___
PM

FRIDAY

HIDING **FISH BEHAVIOUR** ACTIVE
| 1 | 2 | 3 | 4 | 5 |

AM
___
PM

SATURDAY

HIDING **FISH BEHAVIOUR** ACTIVE
| 1 | 2 | 3 | 4 | 5 |

AM
___
PM

SUNDAY

HIDING **FISH BEHAVIOUR** ACTIVE
| 1 | 2 | 3 | 4 | 5 |

AM
___
PM

TEST/ CHANGE / CHECK

/ /	AM PM	°C	DAYS SINCE LAST TEST

TEST

RESULT ☺ ☹

NH₃ AMMONIA	ppm	☺ ☹
NO₂ NITRITE	ppm	☺ ☹
NO₃ NITRATE	ppm	☺ ☹
pH	pH	☺ ☹

CHECK

FILTERS

CHECKED ☐	CLEANED ☐	**OR**	CHANGED ☐

PUMP	CHECKED ☐
AIRLINE	CHECKED ☐
LIGHTING	CHECKED ☐

CHANGE

NOTE WATER CHANGED AFTER TEST AS A PERCENTAGE

%

WATER TEST/ CHANGE NOTES

FISH COUNT

#

WEEK BEGINNING: / /	FEED TIMES

MONDAY *ADD DAILY NOTES AND OBSERVATIONS*

	HIDING	**FISH BEHAVIOUR**	ACTIVE
	1	2 3	4 5

AM
___
PM

TUESDAY

	HIDING	**FISH BEHAVIOUR**	ACTIVE
	1	2 3	4 5

AM
___
PM

WEDNESDAY

	HIDING	**FISH BEHAVIOUR**	ACTIVE
	1	2 3	4 5

AM
___
PM

THURSDAY

	HIDING	**FISH BEHAVIOUR**	ACTIVE
	1	2 3	4 5

AM
___
PM

FRIDAY

	HIDING	**FISH BEHAVIOUR**	ACTIVE
	1	2 3	4 5

AM
___
PM

SATURDAY

	HIDING	**FISH BEHAVIOUR**	ACTIVE
	1	2 3	4 5

AM
___
PM

SUNDAY

	HIDING	**FISH BEHAVIOUR**	ACTIVE
	1	2 3	4 5

AM
___
PM

TEST/ CHANGE / CHECK

/ /	AM PM	°C	DAYS SINCE LAST TEST	

TEST

RESULT ☺ ☹

		☺ ☹
NH₃ AMMONIA	ppm	☺ ☐ ☹ ☐
NO₂ NITRITE	ppm	☺ ☐ ☹ ☐
NO₃ NITRATE	ppm	☺ ☐ ☹ ☐
pH	pH	☺ ☐ ☹ ☐

CHECK

FILTERS

CHECKED ☐	CLEANED ☐	**OR**	CHANGED ☐

PUMP	CHECKED ☐
AIRLINE	CHECKED ☐
LIGHTING	CHECKED ☐

CHANGE   NOTE WATER CHANGED AFTER TEST AS A PERCENTAGE   %

WATER TEST/ CHANGE NOTES

FISH COUNT
#

WEEK BEGINNING: _____ / _____ / _____

MONDAY
ADD DAILY NOTES AND OBSERVATIONS

HIDING	FISH BEHAVIOUR			ACTIVE
1	2	3	4	5

AM

___

PM

TUESDAY

HIDING	FISH BEHAVIOUR			ACTIVE
1	2	3	4	5

AM

___

PM

WEDNESDAY

HIDING	FISH BEHAVIOUR			ACTIVE
1	2	3	4	5

AM

___

PM

THURSDAY

HIDING	FISH BEHAVIOUR			ACTIVE
1	2	3	4	5

AM

___

PM

FRIDAY

HIDING	FISH BEHAVIOUR			ACTIVE
1	2	3	4	5

AM

___

PM

SATURDAY

HIDING	FISH BEHAVIOUR			ACTIVE
1	2	3	4	5

AM

___

PM

SUNDAY

HIDING	FISH BEHAVIOUR			ACTIVE
1	2	3	4	5

AM

___

PM

TEST/ CHANGE / CHECK

/ /	AM PM	°C	DAYS SINCE LAST TEST

TEST

RESULT ☺ ☹

		☺ ☹
NH₃ AMMONIA	ppm	☺ ☹
NO₂ NITRITE	ppm	☺ ☹
NO₃ NITRATE	ppm	☺ ☹
pH	pH	☺ ☹

CHECK

FILTERS

CHECKED ☐	CLEANED ☐	**OR**	CHANGED ☐

PUMP	CHECKED ☐
AIRLINE	CHECKED ☐
LIGHTING	CHECKED ☐

CHANGE   NOTE WATER CHANGED AFTER TEST AS A PERCENTAGE   %

WATER TEST/ CHANGE NOTES

FISH COUNT

#

WEEK BEGINNING: /   /

MONDAY *ADD DAILY NOTES AND OBSERVATIONS*

HIDING	FISH BEHAVIOUR			ACTIVE
1	2	3	4	5

AM
___
PM

TUESDAY

HIDING	FISH BEHAVIOUR			ACTIVE
1	2	3	4	5

AM
___
PM

WEDNESDAY

HIDING	FISH BEHAVIOUR			ACTIVE
1	2	3	4	5

AM
___
PM

THURSDAY

HIDING	FISH BEHAVIOUR			ACTIVE
1	2	3	4	5

AM
___
PM

FRIDAY

HIDING	FISH BEHAVIOUR			ACTIVE
1	2	3	4	5

AM
___
PM

SATURDAY

HIDING	FISH BEHAVIOUR			ACTIVE
1	2	3	4	5

AM
___
PM

SUNDAY

HIDING	FISH BEHAVIOUR			ACTIVE
1	2	3	4	5

AM
___
PM

TEST/ CHANGE / CHECK

/ /		AM PM	°C	DAYS SINCE LAST TEST	

TEST

RESULT ☺ ☹

NH₃ AMMONIA		ppm	☺ ☐	☹ ☐
NO₂ NITRITE		ppm	☺ ☐	☹ ☐
NO₃ NITRATE		ppm	☺ ☐	☹ ☐
pH		pH	☺ ☐	☹ ☐

CHECK

FILTERS

CHECKED ☐	CLEANED ☐	OR	CHANGED ☐

PUMP	CHECKED ☐
AIRLINE	CHECKED ☐
LIGHTING	CHECKED ☐

CHANGE

NOTE WATER CHANGED AFTER TEST AS A PERCENTAGE

%

WATER TEST/ CHANGE NOTES

FISH COUNT

#

WEEK BEGINNING: / /	FEED TIMES

MONDAY *ADD DAILY NOTES AND OBSERVATIONS*

	HIDING **FISH BEHAVIOUR** ACTIVE 1 2 3 4 5	AM ——— PM

TUESDAY

	HIDING **FISH BEHAVIOUR** ACTIVE 1 2 3 4 5	AM ——— PM

WEDNESDAY

	HIDING **FISH BEHAVIOUR** ACTIVE 1 2 3 4 5	AM ——— PM

THURSDAY

	HIDING **FISH BEHAVIOUR** ACTIVE 1 2 3 4 5	AM ——— PM

FRIDAY

	HIDING **FISH BEHAVIOUR** ACTIVE 1 2 3 4 5	AM ——— PM

SATURDAY

	HIDING **FISH BEHAVIOUR** ACTIVE 1 2 3 4 5	AM ——— PM

SUNDAY

	HIDING **FISH BEHAVIOUR** ACTIVE 1 2 3 4 5	AM ——— PM

TEST/ CHANGE / CHECK

| / / | AM PM | °C | DAYS SINCE LAST TEST | |

TEST

RESULT ☺ ☹

		☺ ☐ ☹ ☐
NH₃ AMMONIA	ppm	☺ ☐ ☹ ☐
NO₂ NITRITE	ppm	☺ ☐ ☹ ☐
NO₃ NITRATE	ppm	☺ ☐ ☹ ☐
pH	pH	☺ ☐ ☹ ☐

CHECK

FILTERS

CHECKED ☐	CLEANED ☐	**OR**	CHANGED ☐

PUMP	CHECKED ☐
AIRLINE	CHECKED ☐
LIGHTING	CHECKED ☐

CHANGE   NOTE WATER CHANGED AFTER TEST AS A PERCENTAGE   %

WATER TEST/ CHANGE NOTES

FISH COUNT

#

WEEK BEGINNING: /   /

MONDAY *ADD DAILY NOTES AND OBSERVATIONS*

HIDING	**FISH BEHAVIOUR**			ACTIVE
1	2	3	4	5

AM
___
PM

TUESDAY

HIDING	**FISH BEHAVIOUR**			ACTIVE
1	2	3	4	5

AM
___
PM

WEDNESDAY

HIDING	**FISH BEHAVIOUR**			ACTIVE
1	2	3	4	5

AM
___
PM

THURSDAY

HIDING	**FISH BEHAVIOUR**			ACTIVE
1	2	3	4	5

AM
___
PM

FRIDAY

HIDING	**FISH BEHAVIOUR**			ACTIVE
1	2	3	4	5

AM
___
PM

SATURDAY

HIDING	**FISH BEHAVIOUR**			ACTIVE
1	2	3	4	5

AM
___
PM

SUNDAY

HIDING	**FISH BEHAVIOUR**			ACTIVE
1	2	3	4	5

AM
___
PM

TEST/ CHANGE / CHECK

| / / | AM PM | °C | DAYS SINCE LAST TEST |

TEST

RESULT ☺ ☹

		☺ ☹
NH₃ AMMONIA	ppm	☺ ☐ ☹ ☐
NO₂ NITRITE	ppm	☺ ☐ ☹ ☐
NO₃ NITRATE	ppm	☺ ☐ ☹ ☐
pH	pH	☺ ☐ ☹ ☐

CHECK

FILTERS

| CHECKED ☐ | CLEANED ☐ | OR | CHANGED ☐ |

PUMP	CHECKED ☐
AIRLINE	CHECKED ☐
LIGHTING	CHECKED ☐

CHANGE   NOTE WATER CHANGED AFTER TEST AS A PERCENTAGE   %

WATER TEST/ CHANGE NOTES

FISH COUNT

#

| **WEEK BEGINNING:** / / | **FEED TIMES** |

MONDAY *ADD DAILY NOTES AND OBSERVATIONS*

HIDING **FISH BEHAVIOUR** ACTIVE
| 1 | 2 | 3 | 4 | 5 |

AM
___
PM

TUESDAY

HIDING **FISH BEHAVIOUR** ACTIVE
| 1 | 2 | 3 | 4 | 5 |

AM
___
PM

WEDNESDAY

HIDING **FISH BEHAVIOUR** ACTIVE
| 1 | 2 | 3 | 4 | 5 |

AM
___
PM

THURSDAY

HIDING **FISH BEHAVIOUR** ACTIVE
| 1 | 2 | 3 | 4 | 5 |

AM
___
PM

FRIDAY

HIDING **FISH BEHAVIOUR** ACTIVE
| 1 | 2 | 3 | 4 | 5 |

AM
___
PM

SATURDAY

HIDING **FISH BEHAVIOUR** ACTIVE
| 1 | 2 | 3 | 4 | 5 |

AM
___
PM

SUNDAY

HIDING **FISH BEHAVIOUR** ACTIVE
| 1 | 2 | 3 | 4 | 5 |

AM
___
PM

TEST/ CHANGE / CHECK

/ /	AM PM	°C	DAYS SINCE LAST TEST

TEST

RESULT ☺ ☹

		☺ ☹
NH$_3$ AMMONIA	ppm	☺ ☐ ☹ ☐
NO$_2$ NITRITE	ppm	☺ ☐ ☹ ☐
NO$_3$ NITRATE	ppm	☺ ☐ ☹ ☐
pH	pH	☺ ☐ ☹ ☐

CHECK

FILTERS

CHECKED ☐	CLEANED ☐	**OR**	CHANGED ☐

PUMP	CHECKED ☐
AIRLINE	CHECKED ☐
LIGHTING	CHECKED ☐

CHANGE   NOTE WATER CHANGED AFTER TEST AS A PERCENTAGE   %

WATER TEST/ CHANGE NOTES

FISH COUNT

\#

WEEK BEGINNING: / /	FEED TIMES

MONDAY *ADD DAILY NOTES AND OBSERVATIONS*

	HIDING	**FISH BEHAVIOUR**	ACTIVE
	1	2 3	4 5

AM
___
PM

TUESDAY

	HIDING	**FISH BEHAVIOUR**	ACTIVE
	1	2 3	4 5

AM
___
PM

WEDNESDAY

	HIDING	**FISH BEHAVIOUR**	ACTIVE
	1	2 3	4 5

AM
___
PM

THURSDAY

	HIDING	**FISH BEHAVIOUR**	ACTIVE
	1	2 3	4 5

AM
___
PM

FRIDAY

	HIDING	**FISH BEHAVIOUR**	ACTIVE
	1	2 3	4 5

AM
___
PM

SATURDAY

	HIDING	**FISH BEHAVIOUR**	ACTIVE
	1	2 3	4 5

AM
___
PM

SUNDAY

	HIDING	**FISH BEHAVIOUR**	ACTIVE
	1	2 3	4 5

AM
___
PM

TEST/ CHANGE / CHECK

| / / | AM
PM | °C | DAYS
SINCE
LAST TEST |

TEST

RESULT ☺ ☹

NH₃ AMMONIA	ppm	☺ ☹
NO₂ NITRITE	ppm	☺ ☹
NO₃ NITRATE	ppm	☺ ☹
pH	pH	☺ ☹

CHECK

FILTERS

| CHECKED ☐ | CLEANED ☐ | OR | CHANGED ☐ |

PUMP	CHECKED ☐
AIRLINE	CHECKED ☐
LIGHTING	CHECKED ☐

CHANGE NOTE WATER CHANGED AFTER TEST AS A PERCENTAGE %

WATER TEST/ CHANGE NOTES

FISH COUNT

#

WEEK BEGINNING: / /	FEED TIMES

MONDAY *ADD DAILY NOTES AND OBSERVATIONS*

HIDING	FISH BEHAVIOUR			ACTIVE
1	2	3	4	5

AM

___

PM

TUESDAY

HIDING	FISH BEHAVIOUR			ACTIVE
1	2	3	4	5

AM

___

PM

WEDNESDAY

HIDING	FISH BEHAVIOUR			ACTIVE
1	2	3	4	5

AM

___

PM

THURSDAY

HIDING	FISH BEHAVIOUR			ACTIVE
1	2	3	4	5

AM

___

PM

FRIDAY

HIDING	FISH BEHAVIOUR			ACTIVE
1	2	3	4	5

AM

___

PM

SATURDAY

HIDING	FISH BEHAVIOUR			ACTIVE
1	2	3	4	5

AM

___

PM

SUNDAY

HIDING	FISH BEHAVIOUR			ACTIVE
1	2	3	4	5

AM

___

PM

GENERAL FISHKEEPING NOTES:

GENERAL FISHKEEPING NOTES:

GENERAL FISHKEEPING NOTES:

Printed in Great Britain
by Amazon